C Programming for School Children

First Edition

Yashavant Kanetkar

BPB PUBLICATIONS
B-14, CONNAUGHT PLACE, NEW DELHI-110001

FIRST EDITION 2014

Copyright © BPB Publications, INDIA

ISBN : 978-81-8333-519-5

All Rights Reserved. No part of this publication may be reproduced or distributed in any form or by any means or stored in a database or retrieval system, without the prior written permission of the publisher with the exception that the program listings may be entered, stored and executed in a computer system, but they may not be reproduced for publication.

LIMITS OF LIABILITY AND DISCLAIMER OF WARRANTY

The information contained in this book is true and correct and the best of Author's & Publisher's knowledge. We are committed to serve students with best of our knowledge and resources. We have taken utmost care and attention while editing and printing of this book but Author and Publisher should not be held responsible for errors, omissions and any other unintentional mistake that might have crept in. However, errors brought to our notice shall be gratefully acknowledged and attended to.

All trademarks referred to in the book are acknowledged as properties of their respective owners. This book is written solely for the benefit and guidance of the students.

Distributors:

COMPUTER BOOK CENTRE
12, Shrungar Shopping Centre,
M.G.Road, BENGALURU–560001
Ph: 25587923/25584641

MICRO BOOKS
Shanti Niketan Building,
8, Camac Street, KOLKATA-700017
Ph: 22826518/22826519

BPB PUBLICATIONS
B-14, Connaught Place,
NEW DELHI-110001
Ph: 23325760/43526249

MICRO MEDIA
Shop No. 5, Mahendra Chambers,
150 DN Rd. Next to Capital Cinema,
V.T. (C.S.T.) Station, MUMBAI-400 001
Ph: 22078296/22078297

BPB BOOK CENTRE
376 Old LajpatRai Market,
DELHI-110006
Ph: 23861747

DECCAN AGENCIES
4-3-329, Bank Street,
HYDERABAD-500195
Ph: 24756967/24756400

INFOTECH
G-2, Sidhartha Building,
96 Nehru Place,
NEW DELHI-110019
Ph: 26438245

BUSINESS PROMOTION BUREAU
8/1 Ritchie Street, Mount Road,
CHENNAI-600002
Ph: 28410796/28550491

Published by Manish Jain for BPB Publications, B-14, Connaught Place, New Delhi-110001 and Printed by him at Adinath Printer, New Delhi.

Dedicated to baba
Who couldn't be here to see this day...

About the Author

Through his books and Quest Video Courseware DVDs on C, C++, Data Structures, VC++, .NET, Embedded Systems, etc. Yashavant Kanetkar has created, moulded and groomed lacs of IT careers in the last two decades. Yashavant's books and Quest DVDs have made a significant contribution in creating top-notch IT manpower in India and abroad.

Yashavant's books are globally recognized and millions of students / professionals have benefitted from them. Yashavant's books have been translated into Hindi, Gujarati, Japanese, Korean and Chinese languages. Many of his books are published in India, USA, Japan, Singapore, Korea and China.

Yashavant is a much sought after speaker in the IT field and has conducted seminars/workshops at TedEx, IITs, RECs and global software companies.

Yashavant has recently been honored with the prestigious "Distinguished Alumnus Award" by IIT Kanpur for his entrepreneurial, professional and academic excellence. This award was given to top 50 alumni of IIT Kanpur who have made significant contribution towards their profession and betterment of society in the last 50 years.

In recognition of his immense contribution to IT education in India, he has been awarded the "Best .NET Technical Contributor" and "Most Valuable Professional" awards by Microsoft for 5 successive years.

Yashavant holds a BE from VJTI Mumbai and M.Tech. from IIT Kanpur. Yashavant's current affiliations include being a Director of KICIT Pvt. Ltd. and KSET Pvt. Ltd. He can be reached at kanetkar@kicit.com or through http://www.kicit.com.

Contents

1. **Getting Started** — 1
   - What is C — 2
   - Getting Started with C — 2
     - The C Character Set — 3
     - Constants, Variables and Keywords — 3
     - Types of C Constants — 4
     - Rules for Constructing Integer Constants — 5
     - Rules for Constructing Real Constants — 5
     - Rules for Constructing Character Constants — 6
     - Types of C Variables — 6
     - Rules for Constructing Variable Names — 6
     - C Keywords — 7
   - The First C Program — 7
     - Form of a C Program — 8
     - What is *main( )* — 8
     - Variables and their Usage — 9
     - *printf( )* and its Purpose — 9
     - Compilation and Execution — 10
   - Receiving Input — 11
   - Sample Programs — 12
   - Things to Remember — 15
   - Exercise — 15

2. **C Instructions** — 19
   - Types of C Instructions — 20
   - Type Declaration Instruction — 20
   - Arithmetic Instruction — 20
   - Integer and Float Conversions — 22
   - Type Conversion in Assignments — 23
   - Hierarchy of Operations — 23
   - Control Instructions in C — 24
   - Sample Programs — 25
   - Things to Remember — 27
   - Exercise — 28

3.	**The Decision Control Instruction**	**31**
	Decisions! Decisions!	32
	The *if* Statement	32
	Multiple Statements within *if*	36
	The *if-else* Statement	38
	Nested *if-else* Statements	40
	Use of Logical Operators	41
	The ! Operator	42
	Decisions Using *switch*	43
	Sample Programs	46
	Things to Remember	49
	Exercise	49
4.	**The Loop Control Instruction**	**51**
	Loops	52
	The *while* Loop	52
	The *for* Loop	54
	The *break* Statement	56
	The *continue* Statement	57
	The *do-while* Loop	58
	Sample Programs	59
	Things to Remember	63
	Exercise	63
5.	**Functions**	**65**
	What is a Function?	66
	Passing Values between Functions	72
	Sample Programs	76
	Things to Remember	78
	Exercise	79
6.	**Arrays**	**81**
	What are Arrays?	82
	A Simple Program using Array	83
	More on Arrays	85
	Array Initialization	86
	Bounds Checking	86
	Passing Array Elements to a Function	87
	Two-Dimensional Arrays	87
	Initializing a 2-Dimensional Array	89
	Sample Programs	90

	Things to Remember	92
	Exercise	93
7.	**Strings**	**95**
	What are Strings?	96
	More about Strings	96
	Standard Library String Functions	99
	Two-Dimensional Array of Characters	101
	Things to Remember	102
	Sample Programs	105
	Exercise	105
8.	**Structures**	**107**
	Why use Structures	108
	Declaring a Structure	110
	Accessing Structure Elements	113
	Array of Structures	113
	Additional Features of Structures	115
	Uses of Structures	118
	Things to Remember	119
	Exercise	119
9.	**Graphics Programming**	**121**
	The First Graphics Program	122
	All Lines are not same	124
	Drawing and Filling Shapes	126
	Filling Regular and Non-Regular Shapes	128
	Outputting Text	130
	A Bit of Animation	132
	Things to Remember	135
	Exercise	135

viii

1 Getting Started

- What is C?
- Getting Started with C
    The C Character Set
    Constants, Variables and Keywords
    Types of C Constants
    Rules for Constructing Integer Constants
    Rules for Constructing Real Constants
    Rules for Constructing Character Constants
    Types of C Variables
    Rules for Constructing Variable Names
    C Keywords
- The First C Program
    Form of a C Program
    What is main( )?
    Variables and their Usage
    printf( ) and its Purpose
    Compilation and Execution
- Receiving Input
- Sample Programs
- Things to Remember
- Exercise

Programming is fun! Before we start enjoying it, it would be interesting to find out what really is C, how it came into existence and where is it used. In this Chapter, we would briefly outline these issues.

Four important aspects of any language are the way it stores data, the way it operates upon this data, how it accomplishes input and output and how it lets you control the sequence of execution of instructions in a program. We would discuss the first three of these building blocks in this Chapter.

What is C?

C is a programming language developed at American Telephone and Telegraph Company's Bell Laboratories in 1972. It was designed and written by a man named Dennis Ritchie. Let us now see where C language is used.

(a) Major parts of popular operating systems like Windows, UNIX, Linux and Android are written in C.

(b) Mobile devices like Smart phones and Tablets work on C programming. Common consumer devices like microwave ovens, washing machines and digital cameras use C programs to carry out their functions.

(c) Three Dimensional computer games where the user navigates some object, like say a spaceship and fires bullets at the invaders are created using gaming frameworks like DirectX. These gaming frameworks are built using C language.

(d) C language is also used to build programs which require to very closely interact with the hardware devices.

Getting Started with C

Learning C language is similar to learning English language. The classical method of learning English is to first learn the alphabets used in the language, then learn to combine these alphabets to form words, which, in turn, are combined to form sentences and sentences are combined to form paragraphs.

Learning C is similar and easier. Instead of straight-away learning how to write programs, we must first know what alphabets, numbers and special symbols are used in C, then how using them, constants, variables and keywords are constructed, and finally, how are these combined to form an instruction. A group of instructions would be combined later on to form a program. This is illustrated in the Figure 1.1.

Chapter 1: Getting Started

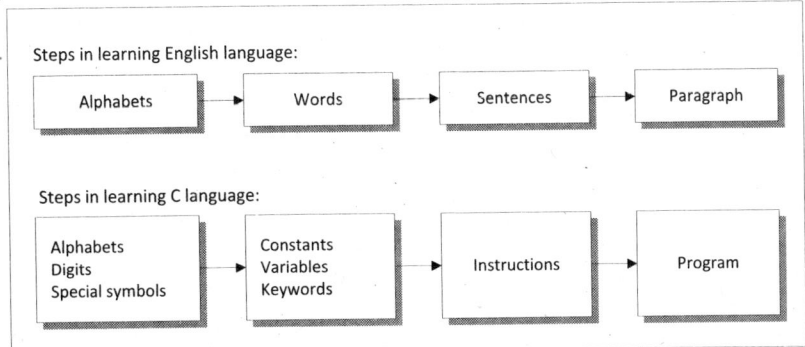

Figure 1.1 Steps in learning English and C Languages

The C Character Set

A character denotes any alphabet, digit or special symbol used to represent information. Figure 1.2 shows the valid alphabets, numbers and special symbols allowed in C.

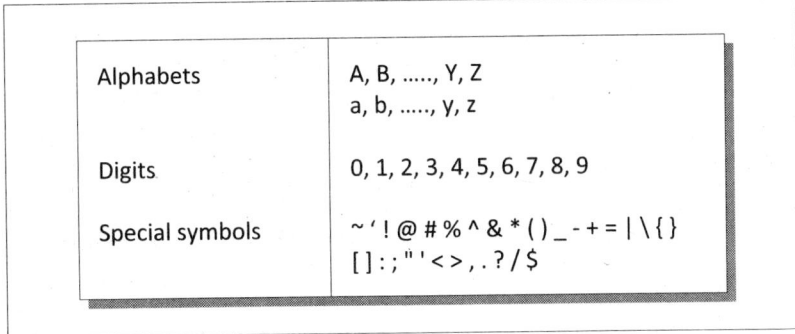

Figure 1.2 C Character set

Constants, Variables and Keywords

The alphabets, digits and special symbols when properly combined form constants, variables and keywords. Let us now understand the meaning of each of them. A constant is an entity that does not change, whereas, a variable is an entity that may change. A keyword is a word that carries special meaning.

In any C program, we typically do lots of calculations. The results of these calculations are stored in computer's memory. Like human memory, the computer's memory also consists of millions of cells. The calculated values are stored in these memory cells. To make the retrieval and usage of these values easy, these memory cells (also called memory locations) are given names. Since the value stored in each location may change, the names given to these locations are called variable names. Let us understand this with the help of an example.

Consider the memory locations shown in Figure 1.3. Here 3 is stored in a memory location and a name **x** is given to it. Then we have assigned a new value 5 to the same memory location **x**. This would overwrite the earlier value 3, since a memory location can hold only one value at a time.

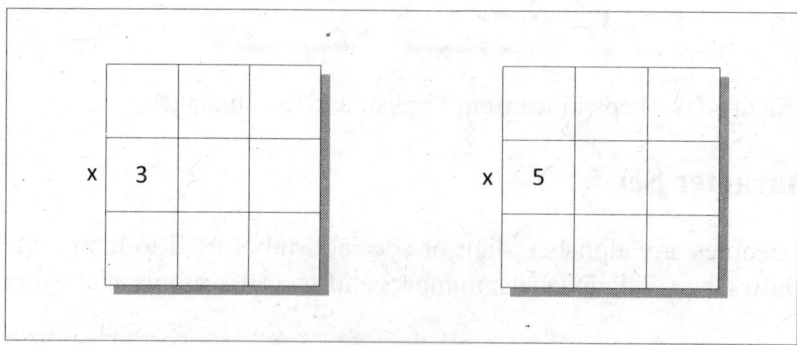

Figure 1.3 Values 3 and 5 stored in Memory Cells

Since the location whose name is **x** can hold different values at different times **x** is known as a variable (or a variable name). As against this, 3 or 5 do not change, hence are known as constants.

Now that we understand the constants and the variables, let us see what different types of constants and variables exist in C.

Types of C Constants

C constants can be divided into two major categories:
(a) Primary Constants
(b) Secondary Constants

These constants are further categorized as shown in Figure 1.4.

Chapter 1: Getting Started

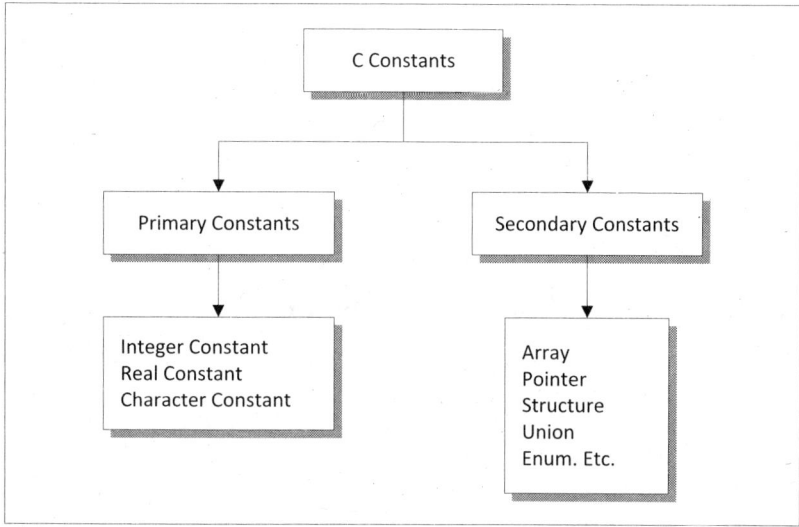

Figure 1.4 Categories of C Constants

At this stage, we would restrict our discussion to only Primary constants, namely, Integer, Real and Character constants. Let us see the details of each of these constants. For constructing these different types of constants, certain rules have been laid down. These rules are as under:

Rules for Constructing Integer Constants

(a) An integer constant must have at least one digit.
(b) It must not have a decimal point.
(c) It can be either positive or negative.
(d) If no sign precedes an integer constant, it is assumed to be positive.
(e) No commas or blanks are allowed within an integer constant.
(f) The allowable range for integer constants is -32768 to +32767.

Examples: 426
 +782
 -8000
 -7605

Rules for Constructing Real Constants

Real constants are often called floating-point constants. Following rules must be observed while constructing real constants expressed in fractional form:

(a) A real constant must have at least one digit.
(b) It must have a decimal point.

(c) It could be either positive or negative.
(d) Default sign is positive.
(e) No commas or blanks are allowed within a real constant.

    Examples: +325.34
                     426.0
                     -32.76
                     -48.5792

Rules for Constructing Character Constants

(a) A character constant is a single alphabet, a single digit or a single special symbol enclosed within single inverted commas.
(b) Both the inverted commas should point to the left. For example, 'A' is a valid character constant whereas 'A' is not.

    Examples: 'A'
                     'I'
                     '5'
                     '='

Types of C Variables

A particular type of variable can hold only the same type of constant. For example, an integer variable can hold only an integer constant, a real variable can hold only a real constant and a character variable can hold only a character constant. The rules for constructing different types of constants are different. However, for constructing variable names of all types, the same set of rules applies. These rules are given below.

Rules for Constructing Variable Names

(a) A variable name is any combination of 1 to 31 alphabets, digits or underscores.
(b) The first character in the variable name must be an alphabet or underscore.
(c) No commas or blanks are allowed within a variable name.
(d) No special symbol other than an underscore (as in **gross_sal**) can be used in a variable name.

    Examples: si_int
                     m_hra
                     pop_e_89

These rules remain same for all the types of primary and secondary variables. Naturally, the question follows—how is C able to differentiate between these variables? This is a rather simple matter. C compiler is able to distinguish between the variable names by making it compulsory for you to declare the type of any variable name that you wish to use in a program. This type declaration is done at the beginning of the program. Following are the examples of type declaration statements:

Ex.: int si, m_hra ;
     float bassal ;
     char code ;

C Keywords

Keywords are the words whose meaning has already been explained to the C compiler (or in a broad sense to the computer). There are only 32 keywords available in C. Figure 1.5 gives a list of these keywords for your ready reference. A detailed discussion of each of these keywords would be taken up in later Chapters wherever their use is relevant.

auto	double	int	struct
break	else	long	switch
case	enum	register	typedef
char	extern	return	union
const	float	short	unsigned
continue	for	signed	void
default	goto	sizeof	volatile
do	if	static	while

Figure 1.5 C Keywords

The First C Program

Once armed with the knowledge of variables, constants and keywords, the next logical step would be to combine them to form instructions. However, instead of this, we would write our first C program now. Once we have done that we would see in detail the instructions that it made use of. The first program is very simple. It calculates simple interest for a set of values representing principle, number of years and rate of interest.

```
/* Calculation of simple interest */
/* Author: gekay  Date: 25/02/2014 */
# include <stdio.h>

int main( )
{
    int  p, n ;
    float  r, si ;
```

```
    p = 1000 ;
    n = 3 ;
    r = 8.5 ;

    /* formula for simple interest */
    si = p * n * r / 100 ;

    printf ( "%f\n" , si ) ;
    return 0 ;
}
```

Let us now understand this program in detail.

Form of a C Program

Form of a C program indicates how it has to be written/typed. There are certain rules about the form of a C program that are applicable to all C programs. These are as under:

(a) Each instruction in a C program is written as a separate statement.

(b) The statements in a program must appear in the same order in which we wish them to be executed; unless of course the logic of the problem demands a deliberate 'jump' or transfer of control to a statement, which is out of sequence.

(c) Blank spaces may be inserted between two words to improve the readability of the statement. However, no blank spaces are allowed within a variable, constant or keyword.

(d) All statements should be in small case letters.

(e) Every C statement must end with a ;. Thus ; acts as a statement terminator.

(f) Comments should be used in a C program to clarify either the purpose of the program or the purpose of some statement in the program.

(g) Comment about the program should be enclosed within /* */. For example, the first two statements in our program are comments.

What is main( )?

main( ) forms the crucial part of any C program. Let us understand its purpose as well as its intricacies.

Chapter 1: Getting Started

main( ) is a function. A function is a set of statements. In a C program, there can be multiple functions. To begin with, we would concentrate only on those programs which have only one function. The name of this function has to be **main( )**, it cannot be anything else. All statements that belong to **main( )** are enclosed within a pair of braces { } as shown below.

```
int main( )
{
    statement 1 ;
    statement 2 ;
    statement 3 ;
}
```

The functions in a calculator return a value, similarly, functions in C also return a value. **main( )** function always returns an integer value, hence there is an **int** before **main( )**. The integer value that we are returning is 0. 0 indicates success. If for any reason the statements in **main( )** fail to do their intended work we can return a non-zero number from **main( )**. This would indicate failure.

Variables and their Usage

We have learnt constants and variables in isolation. Let us understand their significance with reference to our first C program.

(a) Any variable used in the program must be declared before using it. For example,

```
int   p, n ;          /* declaration */
float r, si ;         /* declaration */
si = p * n * r / 100 ;   /* usage */
```

(b) In the statement,

```
si = p * n * r / 100 ;
```

* and / are the arithmetic operators. The arithmetic operators available in C are +, -, * and /.

printf( ) and its Purpose

In C programming to display output on the screen, readymade library functions are used. One such function is **printf( )**. Let us understand this function with respect to our program.

(a) Once the value of **si** is calculated it needs to be displayed on the screen. We have used **printf( )** to do so.

(b) To use the **printf( )** function, it is necessary to use **#include <stdio.h>** at the beginning of the program. **#include** is known as a preprocessor directive.

(c) The general form of **printf( )** function is,

printf ("<format string>", <list of variables>) ;

<format string> can contain,

%f for printing real values
%d for printing integer values
%c for printing character values

In addition to format specifiers like **%f**, **%d** and **%c**, the format string may also contain any other characters. These characters are printed as they are when the **printf( )** is executed.

(d) Given below are some more examples of usage of **printf( )** function:

printf ("%f", si) ;
printf ("%d %d %f %f", p, n, r, si) ;
printf ("Simple interest = Rs. %f", si) ;
printf ("Principal = %d \nRate = %f", p, r) ;

The output of the last statement would look like this

Principal = 1000
Rate = 8.500000

What is '\n' doing in this statement? It is called newline and it takes the cursor to the next line. Therefore, you get the output split over two lines. '\n' comes in handy when we want to format the output properly on separate lines.

Compilation and Execution

Once you have written the program you need to type it and instruct the machine to execute it. To type your C program you need another program called Editor. Once the program has been typed it needs to be converted to machine language (0s and 1s) before the machine can execute it. To carry out this conversion we need another program called Compiler.

Compiler vendors provide an Integrated Development Environment (IDE) which consists of an Editor as well as the Compiler. One such IDE is Turbo C. For creating and executing all programs in this book you can use Turbo C version 2.0 or Turbo C++ version 3.1. If you are using Turbo C or Turbo C++ IDE you can carry out the following steps to get our program executed.

Chapter 1: Getting Started

(a) Start Turbo C IDE at **C>** prompt by typing TC followed by Enter. The Turbo C IDE (TC.EXE) is usually present in **C:\TC\BIN** directory.

(b) Select **New** from the **File** menu.

(c) Type the program.

(d) Save the program using **F2** under a proper name (say Program1.c).

(e) Use **Ctrl + F9** to compile and execute the program.

(f) Use **Alt + F5** to view the output.

A word of caution! If you run this program in Turbo C++ IDE, you may get an error—"The function printf should have a prototype". To get rid of this error, perform the following steps and then recompile the program.

(a) Select **Options** menu and then select **Compiler | C++ Options**. In the dialog box that pops up, select **CPP always** in the **Use C++ Compiler** options.

(b) Again select **Options** menu and then select **Environment | Editor**. Make sure that the default extension is **C** rather than **CPP**.

Receiving Input

In the program discussed above we assumed the values of **p, n** and **r** to be 1000, 3 and 8.5. Every time we run the program we would get the same value for simple interest. If we want to calculate simple interest for some other set of values then we are required to make the relevant changes in the program, and again compile and execute it. Thus the program is not general enough to calculate simple interest for any set of values without being required to make a change in the program.

To make the program general, the program itself should ask the user to supply the values of **p, n** and **r** through the keyboard during execution. This can be achieved using a function called **scanf( )**. This function is a counter-part of the **printf( )** function. **printf( )** outputs the values to the screen whereas **scanf( )** receives them from the keyboard. This is illustrated in the program given below.

```
/* Calculation of simple interest */
/* Author gekay Date 25/02/2014 */
# include <stdio.h>
int main( )
{
    int  p, n ;
    float  r, si ;
```

```
        printf ( "Enter values of p, n, r" ) ;
        scanf ( "%d %d %f", &p, &n, &r ) ;

        si = p * n * r / 100 ;
        printf ( "%f\n" , si ) ;
        return 0 ;
}
```

The first **printf( )** outputs the message 'Enter values of p, n, r' on the screen. Here we have not used any expression in **printf( )** which means that using expressions in **printf( )** is optional.

Note that the ampersand (**&**) before the variables in the **scanf( )** function is a must. **&** is an 'Address of' operator. It gives the location number used by the variable in memory. When we say **&a**, we are telling **scanf( )** at which memory location should it store the value supplied by the user from the keyboard. A blank, a tab or a enter must separate the values supplied to **scanf( )** as shown below.

The three values separated by blank:

 1000 5 15.5

The three values separated by tab:

 1000 5 15.5

The three values separated by enter (newline):

 1000
 5
 15.5

So much for the tips. Given below are a few sample programs that would help you strengthen all the C programming concepts that you have learnt so for.

Sample Programs

(a) Ramesh's basic salary is input through the keyboard. His dearness allowance is 40% of basic salary, and house rent allowance is 20% of basic salary. Write a program to calculate his gross salary.

Program:

Chapter 1: Getting Started

```c
/* Calculate Ramesh's gross salary */
# include <stdio.h>
int main( )
{
    float  bp, da, hra, grpay ;

    printf ( "\nEnter Basic Salary of Ramesh: " ) ;
    scanf ( "%f", &bp ) ;

    da = 0.4 * bp ;
    hra = 0.2 * bp ;
    grpay = bp + da + hra ;  /* Gross Pay = sum of basic & all allowances */

    printf ( "Basic Salary of Ramesh = %f\n ", bp ) ;
    printf ( "Dearness Allowance = %f\n ", da ) ;
    printf ( "House Rent Allowance = %f\n ", hra ) ;
    printf ( "Gross Pay of Ramesh is %f\n", grpay ) ;

    return 0 ;
}
```

(b) The distance between two cities (in km.) is input through the keyboard. Write a program to convert and print this distance in meters, feet, inches and centimeters.

Program:

```c
/* Conversion of distance */
# include <stdio.h>
int main( )
{
    float  km, m , cm, ft, inch ;

    printf ( "\nEnter the distance in Kilometers: " ) ;
    scanf ( "%f", &km ) ;

    m = km * 1000 ;
    cm = m * 100 ;
    inch = cm / 2.54 ;
    ft = inch / 12 ;

    printf ( "Distance in meters = %f\n", m ) ;
    printf ( "Distance in centimeter = %f\n", cm ) ;
    printf ( "Distance in feet = %f\n", ft ) ;
```

```
        printf ( "Distance in inches = % f\n", inch ) ;

        return 0 ;
    }
```

(c) If the marks obtained by a student in five different subjects are input through the keyboard, write a program to find out the aggregate marks and percentage marks obtained by the student. Assume that the maximum marks that can be obtained by a student in each subject is 100.

Program:

```
/* Calculation of aggregate & percentage marks */
# include <stdio.h>
int main( )
{
    int  m1, m2, m3, m4, m5, aggr ;
    float  per ;

    printf ( "\nEnter marks in 5 subjects: " ) ;
    scanf ( "% d % d % d % d % d", &m1, &m2, &m3, &m4, &m5 ) ;

    aggr = m1 + m2 + m3 + m4 + m5 ;
    per = aggr / 5 ;

    printf ( "Aggregate Marks = % d\n", aggr ) ;
    printf ( "Percentage Marks = % f\n", per ) ;

    return 0 ;
}
```

(d) The length & breadth of a rectangle and radius of a circle are input through the keyboard. Write a program to calculate the area and perimeter of the rectangle, and area and circumference of the circle.

Program:

```
/* Calculation of perimeter & area of rectangle and circle */
# include <stdio.h>
int main( )
{
    int  l, b, r, area1, perimeter ;
```

```c
    float area2, circum ;

    printf ( "\nEnter Length & Breadth of Rectangle: " ) ;
    scanf ( "%d %d", &l, &b ) ;
    area1 = l * b ;  /* Area of a rectangle */
    perimeter = 2 * l + 2 * b ;  /* Perimeter of a rectangle */

    printf ( "Area of Rectangle = %d\n", area1 ) ;
    printf ( "Perimeter of Rectangle = %d\n", perimeter) ;

    printf ( "\n\nEnter Radius of circle: " ) ;
    scanf ( "%d", &r ) ;

    area2 = 3.14 * r * r ;  /* Area of Circle */
    circum = 2 * 3.14 * r ;  /* Circumference of a circle */

    printf ( "Area of Circle = %f\n", area2 ) ;
    printf ( "Circumference of Circle = %f\n", circum ) ;

    return 0 ;
}
```

Things to Remember

(a) Constant is an entity whose value remains fixed.
(b) Variable is an entity whose value can change during course of execution of the program.
(c) Keywords are special words whose meaning is known to the Compiler.
(d) There are certain rules which must be followed while building constants or variables.
(e) The three primary constants and variable types in C are integer, float and character.
(f) We should not use a keyword as a variable name.
(g) Comments should be used to indicate the purpose of the program or statements in a program.
(h) Comments can be single line or multi-line.
(i) Input/output in C can be achieved using scanf( ) and **printf( )** functions.

Exercise

[A] Which of the following is invalid C constant and why?

'3.15'   35,550   3.25e2
2e-3   'eLearning'   "show"
'Quest' 2^3 4 6 5 2

[B] Which of the following is invalid variable name and why?

B'day	int	$hello
#HASH	dot.	number
totalArea	_main( )	temp_in_Deg
total%	1st	stack-queue
variable name	%name%	salary in rupees

[C] State whether the following statements are True or False:

(a) C language has been developed by Dennis Ritchie.
(b) Operating systems like Windows, UNIX, Linux and Android are written in C.
(c) C language programs can easily interact with hardware of a PC / Laptop.
(d) A real constant in C can be expressed in both Fractional and Exponential forms.
(e) A character variable can at a time store only one character.
(f) The maximum value that an integer constant can have varies from one compiler to another.
(g) Usually all C statements are written in small case letters.
(h) Spaces may be inserted between two words in a C statement.
(i) Spaces cannot be present within a variable name.
(j) C programs are converted into machine language with the help of a program called Editor.
(k) Most development environments provide an Editor to type a C program and a Compiler to convert it into machine language.
(l) **int, char, float, real, integer, character, char, main, printf** and **scanf** all are keywords.

[D] Match the following:

\n	Literal
3.145	Statement terminator
-6513	Character constant
'D'	Escape sequence
4.25e-3	Input function
main( )	Function
%f, %d, %c	Integer constant
;	Address of operator
Constant	Output function
Variable	Format specifier
&	Output function
printf( )	Real constant
scanf( )	Identifier

Chapter 1: Getting Started

[E] Attempt the following:

(a) Temperature of a city in Fahrenheit degrees is input through the keyboard. Write a program to convert this temperature into Centigrade degrees.

(b) If the total selling price of 15 items and the total profit earned on them is input through the keyboard, write a program to find the cost price of one item.

(c) Paper of size A0 has dimensions 1189 mm x 841 mm. Each subsequent size A(n) is defined as A(n-1) cut in half parallel to its shorter sides. Write a program to calculate and print paper sizes A0, A1, A2, ... A8.

2 C Instructions

- What is C?
- Types of Instructions
- Type Declaration Instruction
- Arithmetic Instruction
- Integer and Float Conversions
- Type of Conversion in Assignment
- Hierarchy of Operations
- Control Instructions in C
- Sample Programs
- Things to Remember
- Exercise

A C program is a set of instructions. The program behaves as per the instructions present in it. Different instructions help us to achieve different tasks in a program. In the last Chapter, we saw how to write simple C programs. In these programs, we used instructions to achieve the intended purpose of the program. In this Chapter, we would explore the details of the instructions that we have used in these programs.

Types of Instructions

There are basically three types of instructions in C:

(a) Type Declaration Instruction – This instruction is used to declare the type of variables used in a C program.

(b) Arithmetic Instruction – This instruction is used to perform arithmetic operations on constants and variables.

(c) Control Instruction – This instruction is used to control the sequence of execution of various statements in a C program.

Type Declaration Instruction

This instruction is used to declare the type of variables being used in the program. Any variable used in the program must be declared before using it in any statement. The type declaration statement is written at the beginning of **main( )** function.

```
Examples:   int bas ;
            float rs, grosssal ;
            char name, code ;
```

While declaring the type of variable we can also initialize it as shown below.

```
int i = 10, j = 25 ;
float a = 1.5, b = 1.99 + 2.4 * 1.44 ;
```

Arithmetic Instruction

A C arithmetic instruction consists of a variable name on the left hand side of = and variable names & constants on the right hand side of =. The variables and constants appearing on the right hand side of = are connected by arithmetic operators like +, -, *, and /.

Examples:

```
int  ad ;
float  kot, deta, alpha, beta, gamma ;
ad = 3200 ;
kot = 0.0056 ;
deta = alpha * beta / gamma + 3.2 * 2 / 5 ;
```

Here,

*, /, -, + are the arithmetic operators.
= is the assignment operator.
2, 5 and 3200 are integer constants.
3.2 and 0.0056 are real constants.
ad is an integer variable.
kot, **deta**, **alpha**, **beta**, **gamma** are real variables.

The variables and constants together are called 'operands'. While executing an arithmetic statement the operands on right hand side are operated upon by the 'arithmetic operators' and the result is then assigned, using the assignment operator, to the variable on left-hand side.

Though Arithmetic instructions look simple to use, one often commits mistakes in writing them. Let us take a closer look at these statements. Note the following points carefully:

(a) C allows only one variable on left-hand side of =. That is, **z = k * l** is legal, whereas **k * l = z** is illegal.

In addition to the division operator, C also provides a modular division operator. This operator returns the remainder on dividing one integer with another. Thus the expression 10 / 2 yields 5, whereas, 10 % 2 yields 0.

An arithmetic instruction is at times used for storing character constants in character variables.

```
char  a, b, d ;
a = 'F' ;
b = 'G' ;
d = '+' ;
```

When we do this, the ASCII (American Standard Code for Information Interchange) values of the characters are stored in the variables. ASCII values are used to represent any character in memory. The ASCII values of 'F' and 'G' are 70 and 71.

(b) Arithmetic operations can be performed on **int**s, **float**s and **char**s.

Thus the statements,

```
char  x, y ;
int  z ;
x = 'a' ;
y = 'b' ;
z = x + y ;
```

are perfectly valid, since the addition is performed on the ASCII values of the characters and not on characters themselves. The ASCII values of 'a' and 'b' are 97 and 98, and hence can definitely be added.

(c) No operator is assumed to be present. It must be written explicitly. In the following example, the multiplication operator after b must be explicitly written.

a = c.d.b(xy)	usual arithmetic statement
b = c * d * b * (x * y)	C statement

Integer and Float Conversions

In order to effectively develop C programs, it will be necessary to understand the rules that are used for the implicit conversion of floating-point and integer values in C. These are mentioned below. Note them carefully.

(a) An arithmetic operation between an integer and integer always yields an integer result.

(b) An operation between a real and real always yields a real result.

(c) An operation between an integer and real always yields a real result. In this operation the integer is first promoted to a real and then the operation is performed. Hence the result is real.

I think a few practical examples shown in Table 2.1 would put the issue beyond doubt.

Chapter 2: C Instructions

Operation	Result	Operation	Result
5 / 2	2	2 / 5	0
5.0 / 2	2.500000	2.0 / 5	0.400000
5 / 2.0	2.500000	2 / 5.0	0.400000
5.0 / 2.0	2.500000	2.0 / 5.0	0.400000

Table 2.1 Results of various operations between an Integer and a Real

Type Conversion in Assignments

It may so happen that the type of the expression and the type of the variable on the left-hand side of the assignment operator may not be the same. In such a case, the value of the expression is promoted or demoted depending on the type of the variable on left-hand side of =.

For example, consider the following assignment statements.

```
int i ;
float b ;
i = 3.5 ;
b = 30 ;
```

Here in the first assignment statement, though the expression's value is a **float** (3.5), it cannot be stored in **i** since it is an **int**. In such a case, the **float** is demoted to an **int** and then its value is stored. Hence what gets stored in **i** is 3. Exactly opposite happens in the next statement. Here, 30 is promoted to 30.000000 and then stored in **b**, since **b** being a **float** variable cannot hold anything except a **float** value.

Hierarchy of Operations

While executing an arithmetic statement, which has two or more operators, we may have some problems as to how exactly does it get executed. For example, does the expression 2 * x - 3 * y correspond to (2x)-(3y) or to 2(x-3y)? Similarly, does A / B * C correspond to A / (B * C) or to (A / B) * C? To answer these questions satisfactorily, one has to understand the 'hierarchy' of operations. The priority or precedence in which the operations in an arithmetic statement are performed is called the hierarchy of operations. The hierarchy of commonly used operators is shown in Table 2.2.

Priority	Operators	Description
1st	* / %	Multiplication, Division, Modular division
2nd	+ -	Addition, Subtraction
3rd	=	Assignment

Table 2.2 Hierarchy of commonly used operators

Within parentheses the same hierarchy as mentioned in Table 2.2 is operative. Also, if there are more than one set of parentheses, the operations within the innermost parentheses would be performed first, followed by the operations within the second innermost pair and so on.

A few examples would clarify the issue further.

Example 2.1: Determine the hierarchy of operations and evaluate the following expression, assuming that **i** is an integer variable:

i = 2 * 3 / 4 + 4 / 4 + 8 - 2 + 5 / 8

Stepwise evaluation of this expression is shown below:

```
i = 2 * 3 / 4 + 4 / 4 + 8 - 2 + 5 / 8
i = 6 / 4 + 4 / 4 + 8 - 2 + 5 / 8        operation: *
i = 1 + 4 / 4 + 8 - 2 + 5 / 8            operation: /
i = 1 + 1+ 8 - 2 + 5 / 8                 operation: /
i = 1 + 1 + 8 - 2 + 0                    operation: /
i = 2 + 8 - 2 + 0                        operation: +
i = 10 - 2 + 0                           operation: +
i = 8 + 0                                operation : -
i = 8                                    operation: +
```

Note that 6 / 4 gives 1 and not 1.5. This so happens because 6 and 4 both are integers and therefore would evaluate to only an integer constant. Similarly 5 / 8 evaluates to zero, since 5 and 8 are integer constants and hence must return an integer value.

Control Instructions in C

As the name suggests, the 'Control Instructions' enable us to specify the order in which the various instructions in a program are to be executed by the computer. In other words,

Chapter 2: C Instructions

the control instructions determine the 'flow of control' in a program. There are four types of control instructions in C. They are:

(a) Sequence Control Instruction
(b) Selection or Decision Control Instruction
(c) Repetition or Loop Control Instruction
(d) Case Control Instruction

The Sequence control instruction ensures that the instructions are executed in the same order in which they appear in the program. Decision and Case control instructions allow the computer to take a decision as to which instruction is to be executed next. The Loop control instruction helps computer to execute a group of statements repeatedly. In the following Chapters, we are going to learn these instructions in detail. Try your hand at the Exercise presented on the following pages before proceeding to the next Chapter, which discusses the decision control instruction.

Sample Programs

(a) If a five-digit number is input through the keyboard, write a program to calculate the sum of its digits. (Hint: Use the modulus operator '%')

Program:

```
/* Sum of digits of a 5 digit number */
# include <stdio.h>
int main( )
{
    int num, a, n ;
    int sum = 0 ; /* initlalize to zero, otherwise it will contain a
                    garbage value*/

    printf ( "\nEnter a 5 digit number(less than 32767): " ) ;
    scanf ( "% d", &num ) ;

    a = num % 10 ;  /* last digit extracted as remainder */
    n = num /10 ;   /* remaining digits */
    sum = sum + a ; /* sum updated with addition of extracted digit */

    a = n % 10 ;    /* 4 th digit */
    n = n /10 ;
    sum = sum + a ;
```

```
        a = n % 10 ;   /* 3 rd digit */
        n = n /10 ;
        sum = sum + a ;

        n = n / 10 ;  /* remaining digits */
        revnum = revnum + a * 100 ;

        a = n % 10 ;   /* 2 nd digit */
        n = n / 10 ;  /* remaining digits */
        revnum = revnum + a * 10 ;

            a = n % 10 ;  /* 1 st digit */
            revnum = revnum + a ;

        /* specifier % ld is used for printing a long integer */
        printf ( "The reversed number is % ld\n", revnum ) ;

            return 0 ;
        }
```

(b) Consider a currency system in which there are notes of seven denominations, namely, ₹ 1, ₹ 2, ₹ 5, ₹ 10, ₹ 50, ₹ 100. If a sum of ₹ N is entered through the keyboard, write a program to compute the smallest number of notes that will combine to give ₹ N.

Program:

```
/* Find smallest number of notes that will combine to give the amount */
# include <stdio.h>

int main( )
{
    int amount, nohun, nofifty, noten, nofive, notwo, noone, totalnotes ;

    printf ( "Enter the amount: " ) ;
    scanf ( "% d", &amount ) ;

    nohun = amount / 100 ;
    amount = amount % 100 ;
    nofifty = amount / 50 ;
    amount = amount % 50 ;
    noten = amount / 10 ;
    amount = amount % 10 ;
```

Chapter 2: C Instructions

```
        nofive = amount / 5 ;
        amount = amount % 5 ;
        notwo = amount / 2 ;
        amount = amount % 2 ;
        noone = amount / 1 ;
        amount = amount % 1 ;

        totalnotes = nohun + nofifty + noten + nofive + notwo + noone ;

        printf ( "Smallest number of notes = %d\n", totalnotes ) ;

        return 0 ;
}
```

(c) If lengths of three sides of a triangle are input through the keyboard, write a program to find the area of the triangle.

Program:

```
/* Find area of a triangle, given its sides */
# include <stdio.h>
# include <math.h>

int main( )
{
    float a, b, c, sp, area ;

    printf ( "\nEnter sides of a triangle: " ) ;
    scanf ( "%f%f%f", &a, &b, &c ) ;

    sp = ( a + b + c ) / 2 ;
    area = sqrt ( sp * ( sp - a ) * ( sp - b ) * ( sp - c ) ) ;
    printf ( "Area of triangle = %f\n", area ) ;

    return 0 ;
}
```

Things to Remember

(a) Instructions in a program control the behavior/working of the program.

(b) A C program can contain three types of instructions—Type declaration instruction, Arithmetic instruction, Control instruction.

(c) An expression may contain any sequence of constants, variables and operators.

(d) An expression is evaluated based on the hierarchy or precedence of operators.

(e) Operators having equal precedence are evaluated using associativity of operators.

(f) Left to right associativity means that the left operand of an operator must be unambiguous; whereas right to left associativity means that the right operand of an operator must be unambiguous.

Exercise

[A] Point out the errors, if any, in the following C statements:

(a) x = (y + 3) ;

(b) cir = 2 * 3.141593 * r ;

(c) char = '3' ;

(d) 4 / 3 * 3.14 * r * r * r = vol_of_sphere ;

(e) volume = a^3 ;

(f) area = 1 / 2 * base * height ;

(g) si = p * r * n / 100 ;

(h) area of circle = 3.14 * r * r ;

[B] State whether the following statements are True or False:

(a) * or /, + or − represents the correct hierarchy of arithmetic operators in C.

(b) [ ] and { } can be used in arithmetic instructions.

(c) Hierarchy decides which operator is used first.

(d) In C, arithmetic instruction cannot contain constants on left side of =.

(e) In C, ** operator is used for exponentiation operation.

(f) % operator cannot be used with floats.

[C] Fill in the blanks:

(a) In y = 10 * x / 2 + z ; ___ operation will be performed first.

(b) If **a** is an integer variable, a = 11 / 2 ; will store ___ in **a**.

(c) The expression, a = 22 / 7 * 5 / 3 ; would evaluate to _____.

(d) The expression, a = 5000 * 3 + 6754 ; would evaluate to ___.

(e) The expression x = -7 % 2 - 8 ; would evaluate to ___.

(f) If **d** is a **float** the operation **d = 2 / 7.0** would store ___ in **d**.

[D] Attempt the following:

(a) If a five-digit number is input through the keyboard, write a program to reverse the number.

(b) If a four-digit number is input through the keyboard, write a program to obtain the sum of the first and last digit of this number.

(c) Wind chill factor is the felt air temperature on exposed skin due to wind. The wind chill temperature is always lower than the air temperature, and is calculated as per the following formula:

wcf = 35.74 + 0.6215t + (0.4275t - 35.75) * $v^{0.16}$

Write a program to receive values of temperature (t) and wind velocity (v) and calculate wind chill factor (wcf).

3 Decision Control Instruction

- Decisions! Decisions!
- The if Statement
    Multiple Statements within if
- The if-else Statement
    Nested if-else Statements
- Use of Logical Operators
    The ! Operator
- Decisions using switch
- Sample Programs
- Things to Remember
- Exercise

We all need to alter our actions in the face of changing circumstances. If the weather is fine, then I will go for a stroll. If the highway is busy, I would take a diversion. If the pitch takes spin, we would win the match. If you like this book, I would write the next edition. You can notice that all these decisions depend on some condition being met.

C language too must be able to perform different sets of actions depending on the circumstances. C has three major decision making instructions—the **if** statement, the **if-else** statement, and the **switch** statement. In this Chapter, we will explore all these ways in which a C program can react to changing circumstances.

Decisions! Decisions!

In the programs written in Chapters 1 and 2, we have used sequence control structure in which the various steps are executed sequentially, i.e., in the same order in which they appear in the program. In fact, to execute the instructions sequentially, we do not have to do anything at all. That is, by default, the instructions in a program are executed sequentially. However, in serious programming situations, seldom do we want the instructions to be executed sequentially. Many a time, we want a set of instructions to be executed in one situation, and an entirely different set of instructions to be executed in another situation. This kind of situation is dealt with in C programs using a decision control instruction. As mentioned earlier, a decision control instruction can be implemented in C using:

(a) The **if** statement
(b) The **if-else** statement
(c) The conditional operators

Now let us learn each of these and their variations in turn.

The if Statement

C uses the keyword **if** to implement the decision control instruction. The general form of **if** statement looks like this:

```
if ( this condition is true )
    execute this statement ;
```

The keyword **if** tells the compiler that what follows is a decision control instruction. The condition following the keyword **if** is always enclosed within a pair of parentheses. If the condition, whatever it is, is true, then the statement is executed. If the condition is not true, then the statement is not executed; instead the program skips past it. But how do we

Chapter 3: Decision Control Instruction **33**

express the condition itself in C? And how do we evaluate its truth or falsity? As a general rule, we express a condition using C's 'relational' operators. The relational operators allow us to compare two values to see whether they are equal to each other, unequal, or whether one is greater than the other. Here's how they look and how they are evaluated in C.

this expression	is true if
x == y	x is equal to y
x != y	x is not equal to y
x < y	x is less than y
x > y	x is greater than y
x <= y	x is less than or equal to y
x >= y	x is greater than or equal to y

Table 3.1 Expressions using Relational Operators and their Results

The relational operators should be familiar to you except for the equality operator == and the inequality operator !=. Note that = is used for assignment, whereas, == is used for comparison of two quantities. Here is a simple program, which demonstrates the use of **if** and the relational operators.

```
/* Demonstration of if statement */
# include <stdio.h>
int main( )
{
    int  num ;

    printf ( "Enter a number less than 10 " ) ;
    scanf ( "%d", &num ) ;

    if ( num < 10 )
        printf ( "You have entered a value which is less than 10\n" ) ;

    return 0 ;
}
```

On execution of this program, if you type a number less than 10, you get a message on the screen through **printf( )**. If you type some other number the program does not do anything. The flowchart given in Figure 3.1 would help you to understand the flow of control in the program.

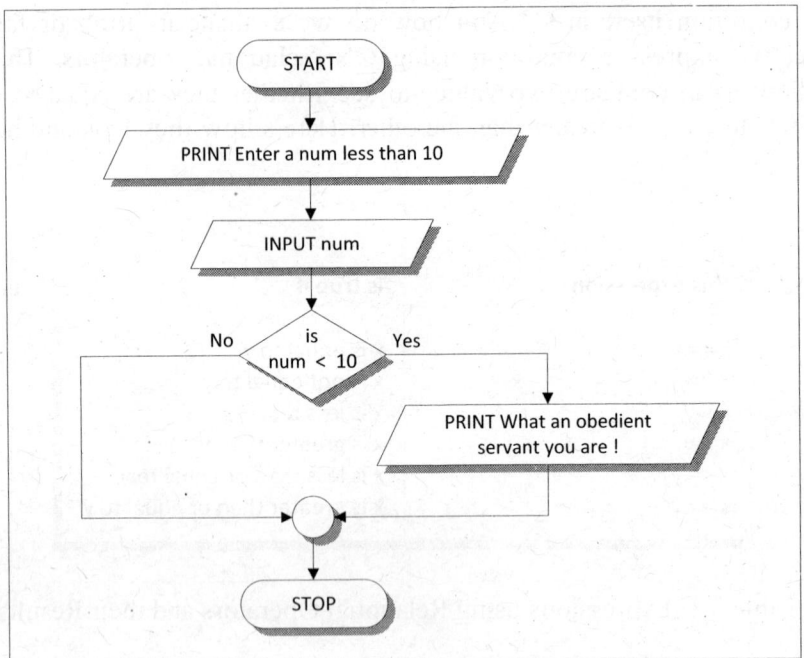

Figure 3.1 Flowchart for Demonstration of if statement

To make you comfortable with the decision control instruction, one more example has been given below. Study it carefully before reading further. To help you to understand it easily, the program is accompanied by an appropriate flowchart.

Example 3.1: While purchasing certain items, a discount of 10% is offered if the quantity purchased is more than 1000. If quantity and price per item are input through the keyboard, write a program to calculate the total expenses.

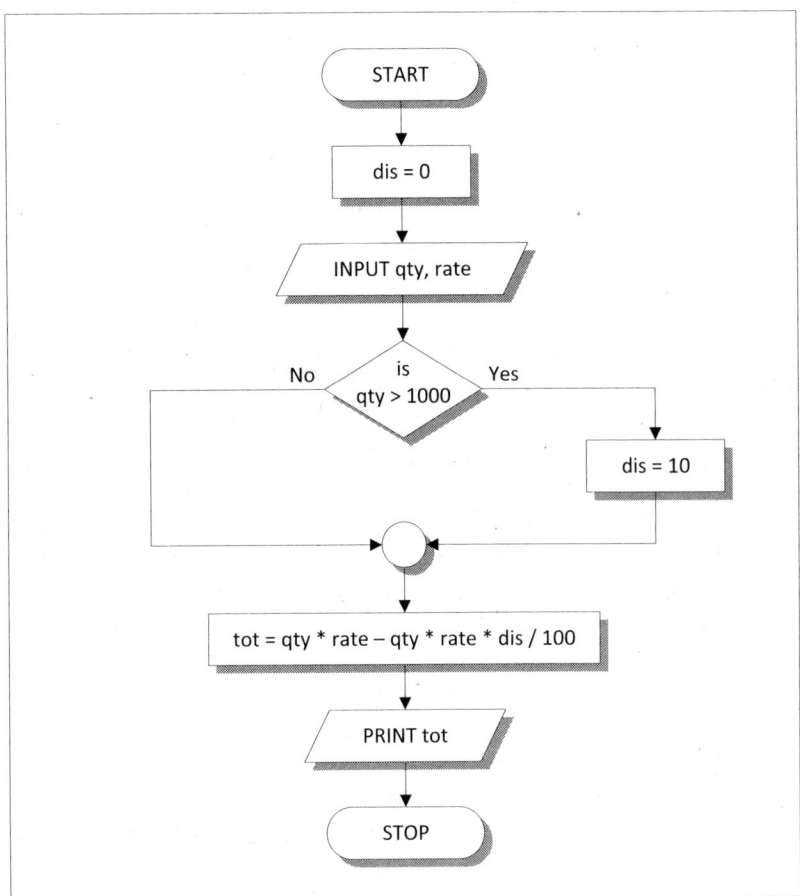

Figure 3.2 Flowchart for Calculation of Total Expenses

```
/* Calculation of total expenses */
# include <stdio.h>
int main( )
{
    int   qty, dis = 0 ;
    float  rate, tot ;
    printf ( "Enter quantity and rate " ) ;
    scanf ( "%d %f", &qty, &rate) ;

    if ( qty > 1000 )
        dis = 10 ;

    tot = ( qty * rate ) - ( qty * rate * dis / 100 ) ;
    printf ( "Total expenses = Rs. %f\n", tot ) ;
    return 0 ;
```

}

Here is some sample interaction with the program.

Enter quantity and rate 1200 15.50
Total expenses = Rs. 16740.000000

Enter quantity and rate 200 15.50
Total expenses = Rs. 3100.000000

In the first run of the program, the condition evaluates to true, as 1200 (value of **qty**) is greater than 1000. Therefore, the variable **dis**, which was earlier set to 0, now gets a new value 10. Using this new value, total expenses are calculated and printed.

In the second run, the condition evaluates to false, as 200 (the value of **qty**) is not greater than 1000. Thus, **dis**, which is earlier set to 0, remains 0, and hence the expression after the minus sign evaluates to zero, thereby offering no discount.

Is the statement **dis = 0** necessary? The answer is yes, since in C, a variable, if not specifically initialized, contains some unpredictable value (garbage value).

Multiple Statements within if

It may so happen that in a program we want more than one statement to be executed if the expression following **if** is satisfied. If such multiple statements are to be executed, then they must be placed within a pair of braces, as illustrated in the following example:

Example 3.2: The current year and the year in which the employee joined the organization are entered through the keyboard. If the number of years for which the employee has served the organization is greater than 3, then a bonus of ₹ 2500/- is given to the employee. If the years of service are not greater than 3, then the program should do nothing.

```
/* Calculation of bonus */
# include <stdio.h>
int main( )
{
    int  bonus, cy, yoj, yos ;

    printf ( "Enter current year and year of joining " ) ;
    scanf ( "%d %d", &cy, &yoj ) ;
```

Chapter 3: Decision Control Instruction 37

```
    yos = cy - yoj ;

    if ( yos > 3 )
    {
        bonus = 2500 ;
        printf ( "Bonus = Rs. %d\n", bonus ) ;
    }
    return 0 ;
}
```

Observe that here the two statements to be executed on satisfaction of the condition have been enclosed within a pair of braces. If a pair of braces is not used, then the C compiler assumes that the programmer wants only the immediately next statement after the **if** to be executed on satisfaction of the condition. In other words, we can say that the default scope of the **if** statement is the immediately next statement after it. Figure 3.3 shows the flowchart to calculate and print bonus value using **if** statement.

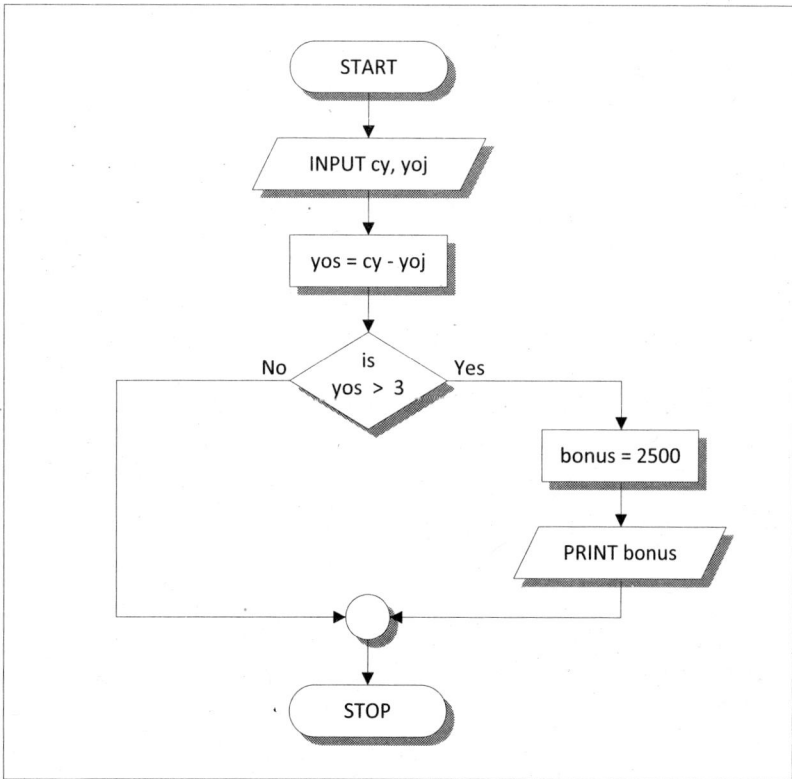

Figure 3.4 Flowchart to Calculate and Print Bonus

The if-else Statement

The **if** statement by itself will execute a single statement, or a group of statements, when the expression following **if** evaluates to true. It does nothing when the expression evaluates to false. Can we execute one group of statements if the expression evaluates to true and another group of statements if the expression evaluates to false? Of course! This is what is the purpose of the **else** statement that is demonstrated in the following example.

Example 3.3: In a company an employee is paid as under:

If his basic salary is less than ₹. 1500, then HRA = 10% of basic salary and DA = 90% of basic salary. If his salary is either equal to or above ₹ 1500, then HRA = ₹ 500 and DA = 98% of basic salary. If the employee's salary is input through the keyboard write a program to find his gross salary.

```
/* Calculation of gross salary */
# include <stdio.h>
int main( )
{
    float  bs, gs, da, hra ;

    printf ( "Enter basic salary " ) ;
    scanf ( "%f", &bs ) ;

    if ( bs < 1500 )
    {
        hra = bs * 10 / 100 ;
        da = bs * 90 / 100 ;
    }
    else
    {
        hra = 500 ;
        da = bs * 98 / 100 ;
    }

    gs = bs + hra + da ;
    printf ( "gross salary = Rs. %f\n", gs ) ;
    return 0 ;
}
```

Figure 3.4 illustrates the flowchart to calculate groos salary using **if-else** statement.

Chapter 3: Decision Control Instruction **39**

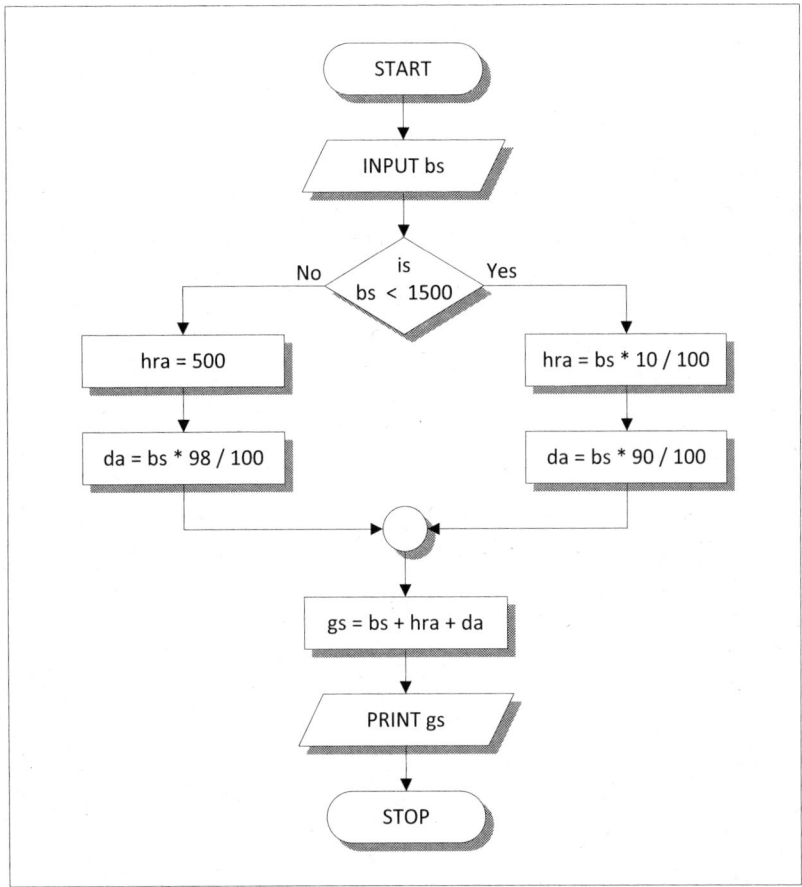

Figure 3.5 Flowchart for Calculation of Gross Salary using **if-else** Statement

A few points worth noting...

(a) The group of statements after the **if** upto and not including the **else** is called an 'if block'. Similarly, the statements after the **else** form the 'else block'.

(b) Notice that the **else** is written exactly below the **if**. The statements in the if block and those in the else block have been indented to the right. This formatting convention is followed throughout the book to enable you to understand the working of the program better.

(c) Had there been only one statement to be executed in the if block and only one statement in the else block we could have dropped the pair of braces.

(d) As with the **if** statement, the default scope of **else** is also the statement immediately after the **else**. To override this default scope, a pair of braces, as shown in the above example, must be used.

Nested if-else Statements

It is perfectly all right if we write an entire **if-else** construct within either the body of the **if** statement or the body of an **else** statement. This is called 'nesting'of **if**s. This is shown in the following program:

```
/* A quick demo of nested if-else */
# include <stdio.h>
int main( )
{
    int  i ;

    printf ( "Enter either 1 or 2 " ) ;
    scanf ( "%d", &i ) ;

    if ( i == 1 )
        printf ( "You would go to heaven !\n" ) ;
    else
    {
        if ( i == 2 )
            printf ( "Hell was created with you in mind\n" ) ;
        else
            printf ( "How about mother earth !\n" ) ;
    }

    return 0 ;
}
```

Note that the second **if-else** construct is nested in the first **else** statement. If the condition in the first **if** statement is false, then the condition in the second **if** statement is checked. If it is false as well, then the final **else** statement is executed.

You can see in the program how each time a **if-else** construct is nested within another **if-else** construct, it is also indented to add clarity to the program. Inculcate this habit of indentation; otherwise, you would end up writing programs which nobody (you included) can understand easily at a later date. Note that whether we indent or do not indent the program, it does not alter the flow of execution of instructions in the program.

Chapter 3: Decision Control Instruction

In the above program, an **if-else** occurs within the **else** block of the first **if** statement. Similarly, in some other program, an **if-else** may occur in the **if** block as well. There is no limit on how deeply the **if**s and the **else**s can be nested.

Use of Logical Operators

C allows usage of three logical operators, namely, &&, || and !. These are to be read as 'AND' 'OR' and 'NOT', respectively.

There are several things to note about these logical operators. Most obviously, two of them are composed of double symbols: || and &&.

The first two operators, && and ||, allow two or more conditions to be combined in an **if** statement. Let us see how they are used in a program. Consider the following example:

Example 3.4: The marks obtained by a student in 5 different subjects are input through the keyboard. The student gets a division as per the following rules:

Percentage above or equal to 60 - First division
Percentage between 50 and 59 - Second division
Percentage between 40 and 49 - Third division
Percentage less than 40 - Fail

Write a program to calculate the division obtained by the student.

```
# include <stdio.h>
int main( )
{
    int m1, m2, m3, m4, m5, per ;

    printf ( "Enter marks in five subjects " ) ;
    scanf ( "%d %d %d %d %d", &m1, &m2, &m3, &m4, &m5 ) ;

    per = ( m1 + m2 + m3 + m4 + m5 ) / 500 * 100 ;

    if ( per >= 60 )
        printf ( "First division\n" ) ;

    if ( ( per >= 50 ) && ( per < 60 ) )
        printf ( "Second division\n" ) ;

    if ( ( per >= 40 ) && ( per < 50 ) )
        printf ( "Third division\n" ) ;
```

```
    if ( per < 40 )
        printf ( "Fail\n" ) ;

    return 0 ;
}
```

As can be seen from the second **if** statement, the **&&** operator is used to combine two conditions. 'Second division' gets printed if both the conditions evaluate to true. If one of the conditions evaluate to false then the whole thing is treated as false.

The ! Operator

So far we have used only the logical operators **&&** and **||**. The third logical operator is the NOT operator, written as **!**. This operator reverses the result of the expression it operates on. For example, if the expression evaluates to a non-zero value, then applying **!** operator to it results into a 0. Vice versa, if the expression evaluates to zero then on applying **!** operator to it makes it 1, a non-zero value. The final result (after applying **!**) 0 or 1 is considered to be false or true, respectively. Here is an example of the NOT operator applied to a relational expression.

! (y < 10)

This means "not **y** less than 10". In other words, if **y** is less than 10, the expression will be false, since **(y < 10)** is true. We can express the same condition as **(y >= 10)**.

The NOT operator is often used to reverse the logical value of a single variable, as in the following expression:

if (! flag)

Following is another way of saying:

if (flag == 0)

Does the NOT operator sound confusing? Avoid it if you want, as the same thing can be achieved without using the NOT operator.

Table 3.2 summarizes the working of all the three logical operators.

Chapter 3: Decision Control Instruction

Operands		Results			
x	y	!x	!y	x && y	x || y
0	0	1	1	0	0
0	non-zero	1	0	0	1
non-zero	0	0	1	0	1
non-zero	non-zero	0	0	1	1

Table 3.2 Results using Operands and Logical Operators

Decisions using switch

The control statement that allows us to make a decision from the number of choices is called a **switch**, or more correctly a **switch-case-default**, since these three keywords go together to make up the control statement. They most often appear as follows:

```
switch ( integer expression )
{
    case constant 1 :
        do this ;
    case constant 2 :
        do this ;
    case constant 3 :
        do this ;
    default :
        do this ;
}
```

The integer expression following the keyword **switch** is any C expression that will yield an integer value. It could be an integer constant like 1, 2 or 3, or an expression that evaluates to an integer. The keyword **case** is followed by an integer or a character constant. Each constant in each **case** must be different from all the others. The "do this" lines in the above form of **switch** represent any valid C statement.

What happens when we run a program containing a **switch**? First, the integer expression following the keyword **switch** is evaluated. The value it gives is then matched, one by one, against the constant values that follow the **case** statements. When a match is found, the program executes the statements following that **case**, and all subsequent **case** and

default statements as well. If no match is found with any of the **case** statements, only the statements following the **default** are executed. A few examples will show how this control instruction works.

Consider the following program:

```
# include <stdio.h>
int main( )
{
    int  i = 2 ;

    switch ( i )
    {
        case 1 :
            printf ( "I am in case 1 \n" ) ;
        case 2 :
            printf ( "I am in case 2 \n" ) ;
        case 3 :
            printf ( "I am in case 3 \n" ) ;
        default :
            printf ( "I am in default \n" ) ;
    }
    return 0 ;
}
```

The output of this program would be:

I am in case 2
I am in case 3
I am in default

The output is definitely not what we expected! We did not expect the second and third line in the above output. The program prints case 2 and case 3 and the default case. Well, yes. We said the **switch** executes the case where a match is found and all the subsequent **cases** and the **default** as well.

If you want that only case 2 should get executed, it is upto you to get out of the **switch** then and there by using a **break** statement. The following example shows how this is done. Note that there is no need for a **break** statement after the **default**, since on reaching the **default** case, the control comes out of the **switch** anyway.

```
# include <stdio.h>
int main( )
```

```
{
    int  i = 2 ;
    switch ( i )
    {
        case 1 :
            printf ( "I am in case 1 \n" ) ;
            break ;
        case 2 :
            printf ( "I am in case 2 \n" ) ;
            break ;
        case 3 :
            printf ( "I am in case 3 \n" ) ;
            break ;
        default :
            printf ( "I am in default \n" ) ;
    }
    return 0 ;
}
```

The output of this program would be:

I am in case 2

The operation of **switch** is shown in Figure 3.5 in the form of a flowchart for a better understanding.

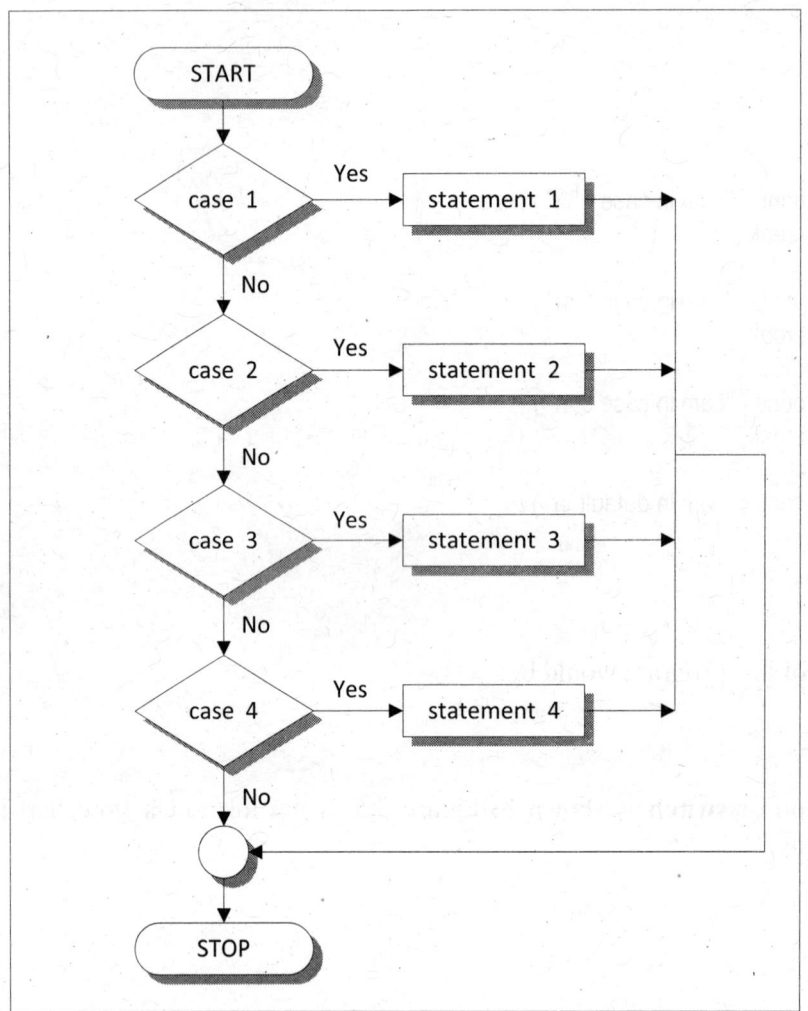

Figure 3.5 Flowchart for **switch** statement

Sample Programs

(a) A five-digit number is entered through the keyboard. Write a program to obtain the reversed number and to determine whether the original and reversed numbers are equal or not.

Program:

/* Check whether a number and its reversed number are equal */

```c
# include <stdio.h>
int main( )
{
    int  n, a, b, num ;
    long int  revnum = 0 ;

    printf ( "\nEnter a five digit number (less than or equal to 32767): " ) ;
    scanf ( "%d", &n ) ;

    num = n ;
    a = n % 10 ;  /* last digit */
    n = n / 10 ;  /* remaining digits */
    revnum = revnum + a * 10000L;

    a = n % 10 ;  /* 4 th digit */
    n = n / 10 ;  /* remaining digits */
    revnum = revnum + a * 1000;

    a = n % 10 ;  /* 3 rd digit */
    n = n / 10 ;  /* remaining digits */
    revnum = revnum + a * 100;

    a = n % 10 ;  /* 2 nd digit */
    n = n / 10 ;  /* remaining digits */
    revnum = revnum + a * 10 ;

    a = n % 10 ;  /* 1 st digit */
    revnum = revnum + a ;

    if ( revnum == num )
        printf ( "Given number & its reversed number are equal\n" ) ;
    else
        printf ( "Given number & its reversed number are not equal\n" ) ;

    return 0 ;
}
```

(b) Given the length and breadth of a rectangle, write a program to find whether the area of the rectangle is greater than its perimeter. For example, the area of the rectangle with length = 5 and breadth = 4 is greater than its perimeter.

Program:

```
/* Find whether area of rectangle is greater than its perimeter */
# include <stdio.h>
int main( )
{
    int l, b, area, peri ;

    printf ( "\nEnter length and breadth of the rectangle: " ) ;
    scanf ( "%d %d", &l, &b ) ;

    area = l * b ;
    peri = 2 * ( l + b ) ;

    if ( area > peri )
        printf ( "area is greater than perimeter\n" ) ;
    else
        printf ( "area is lesser than perimeter\n" ) ;

    return 0 ;
}
```

(c) Given three points **(x1, y1), (x2, y2)** and **(x3, y3)**, write a program to check if all the three points fall on one straight line.

Program:

```
/* Check whether three points are co-linear */
# include <stdio.h>
# include <math.h>
int main( )
{
    int x1, y1, x2, y2, x3, y3 ;
    int s1, s2, s3 ;

    printf ( "\nEnter the values of x1 and y1 coordinates of first point: " ) ;
    scanf ( "%d %d", &x1, &y1 ) ;
    printf ( "\nEnter the values of x2 and y2 coordinates of first point: " ) ;
    scanf ( "%d %d", &x2, &y2 ) ;
    printf ( "\nEnter the values of x3 and y3 coordinates of first point: " ) ;
    scanf ( "%d %d", &x3, &y3 ) ;

    /* Calculate Slope of line between each pair of points */
    s1 = abs ( x2 - x1 ) / abs ( y2 - y1 ) ;
    s2 = abs ( x3 - x1 ) / abs ( y3 - y1 ) ;
```

Chapter 3: Decision Control Instruction **49**

```
        s3 = abs ( x3 - x2 ) / abs ( y3 - y2 ) ;

        if ( ( s1 == s2 ) && ( s1 == s3 ) )
            printf ( "Points are Co-linear\n" ) ;
        else
            printf ( "Points are NOT Co-linear\n" ) ;

        return 0 ;
    }
```

Things to Remember

(a) There are two ways for taking decisions in a program. First way is to use the **if-else** statement, second way is to use the **switch** statement.

(b) The default scope of **if** statement is only the next statement. So, to execute more than one statement they must be written in a pair of braces.

(c) An **if** block need not always be associated with an **else** block. However, an **else** block must always be associated with an **if**.

(d) **&&** and **||** are binary operators, whereas, **!** is a unary operator.

(e) When we need to choose one amongst number of alternatives, a **switch** statement is used.

(f) The control falls through all the cases unless the fall is stopped using a **break** statement.

Exercise

[A] State whether the following statements are True or False:

(a) A decision control instruction can be implemented in C using either **if** statement or **if-else** statement.

(b) The == operator is used for assignment, whereas = operator is used for comparison of two quantities.

(c) **switch** can be used to check integer expressions only.

[B] Fill in the blanks:

(a) By default, the instructions in a C program are executed _____.

(b) The condition following the keyword _____ is always enclosed within a pair of parentheses.

(c) The _____ operator reverses the result of the expression it operates on.

[C] Attempt the following:

(a) Given a point **(x, y)**, write a program to find out if it lies on the X-axis, Y-axis or on the origin, viz. (0, 0).

(b) If the three sides of a triangle are entered through the keyboard, write a program to check whether the triangle is valid or not. The triangle is valid if the sum of two sides is greater than the largest of the three sides.

(c) If the three sides of a triangle are entered through the keyboard, write a program to check whether the triangle is isosceles, equilateral, scalene or right angled triangle.

4 Loop Control Instruction

- What is C?
- Loops
- The while Loop
- The for Loop
- The break Statement
- The continue Statement
- The do-while Loop
- Sample Programs
- Things to Remember
- Exercise

The programs that we have developed so far used either a sequential or a decision control instruction. In the first one, the calculations were carried out in a fixed order; while in the second, an appropriate set of instructions were executed depending upon the outcome of the condition being tested (or a logical decision being taken).

These programs were of limited nature, because when executed, they always performed the same series of actions, in the same way, exactly once. Almost always, if something is worth doing, it is worth doing more than once. You can probably think of several examples of this from real life, such as eating a good dinner or going for a movie. Programming is the same; we frequently need to perform an action over and over, often with variations in the details each time. The mechanism, which meets this need, is the 'loop', and loops are the subject of this Chapter.

Loops

The versatility of the computer lies in its ability to perform a set of instructions repeatedly. This involves repeating some portion of the program either a specified number of times or until a particular condition is being satisfied. This repetitive operation is done through a loop control instruction.

There are three methods by way of which we can repeat a part of a program. They are:

Using a **for** statement
Using a **while** statement
Using a **do-while** statement

Each of these methods is discussed in the following sections.

The while Loop

It is often the case in programming that you want to do something a fixed number of times. Perhaps you want to calculate gross salaries of ten different persons, or you want to convert temperatures from Centigrade to Fahrenheit for 15 different cities. The **while** loop is ideally suited for this.

Let us look at a simple example, which uses a **while** loop. The flowchart shown in Figure 4.1 would help you to understand the operation of the **while** loop.

Chapter 4: Loop Control Instruction

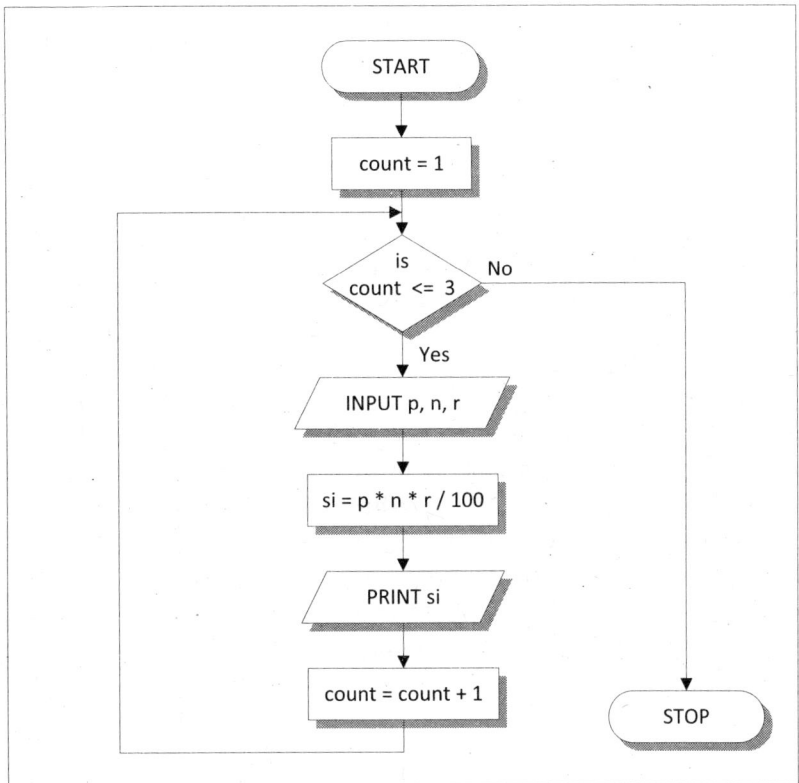

Figure 4.1 Flowchart using while Loop

```
/* Calculation of simple interest for 3 sets of p, n and r */
# include <stdio.h>
int main( )
{
    int   p, n, count ;
    float  r, si ;

    count = 1 ;
    while ( count <= 3 )
    {
        printf ( "\nEnter values of p, n and r " ) ;
        scanf ( "% d % d % f", &p, &n, &r ) ;
        si = p * n * r / 100 ;
        printf ( "Simple interest = Rs. % \nf", si ) ;

        count = count + 1 ;
    }
```

       return 0 ;
}

And here are a few sample runs of the program...

Enter values of p, n and r 1000 5 13.5
Simple interest = Rs. 675.000000
Enter values of p, n and r 2000 5 13.5
Simple interest = Rs. 1350.000000
Enter values of p, n and r 3500 5 3.5
Simple interest = Rs. 612.500000

The program executes all statements after the **while** 3 times. The logic for calculating the simple interest is written within a pair of braces immediately after the **while** keyword. These statements form the 'body' of the **while** loop. The parentheses after the **while** contain a condition. So long as this condition remains true, all statements within the body of the **while** loop keep getting executed repeatedly. To begin with, the variable **count** is initialized to 1 and every time the simple interest logic is executed, the value of **count** is incremented by one. The variable **count** is many a time called either a 'loop counter' or an 'index variable'.

The for Loop

Perhaps one reason why few programmers use **while** is that they are too busy using the **for**, which is probably the most popular looping instruction. The **for** allows us to specify three things about a loop in a single line:

(a) Setting a loop counter to an initial value.
(b) Testing the loop counter to determine whether its value has reached the number of repetitions desired.
(c) Increasing the value of loop counter each time the program segment within the loop has been executed.

The general form of **for** statement is as under:

```
for ( initialize counter ; test counter ; increment counter )
{
    do this ;
    and this ;
    and this ;
}
```

Chapter 4: Loop Control Instruction

Note that we cannot use commas in place semicolons in the for statement.

Let us write down the simple interest program using **for**. Compare this program with the one, which we wrote using **while**. The flowchart is also given in Figure 4.2 for a better understanding.

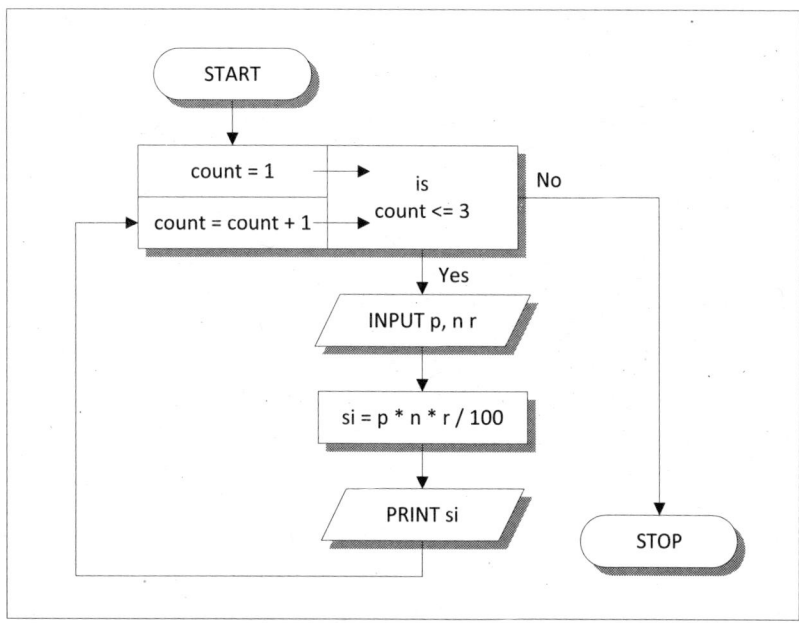

Figure 4.2 Flowchart using for Loop

```
/* Calculation of simple interest for 3 sets of p, n and r */
# include <stdio.h>
int main( )
{
    int   p, n, count ;
    float  r, si ;

    for ( count = 1 ; count <= 3 ; count = count + 1 )
    {
        printf ( "Enter values of p, n, and r " ) ;
        scanf ( "%d %d %f", &p, &n, &r ) ;

        si = p * n * r / 100 ;
        printf ( "Simple Interest = Rs.%f\n", si ) ;
    }
    return 0 ;
}
```

If you compare this program with the one written using **while**, you can observe that the three steps—initialization, testing and incrementation—required for the loop construct have now been incorporated in the **for** statement.

Let us now examine how the **for** statement gets executed:

- When the **for** statement is executed for the first time, the value of **count** is set to an initial value 1.
- Now the condition **count <= 3** is tested. Since **count** is 1, the condition is satisfied and the body of the loop is executed for the first time.
- Upon reaching the closing brace of **for**, control is sent back to the **for** statement, where the value of **count** gets incremented by 1.
- Again the test is performed to check whether the new value of **count** exceeds 3.
- If the value of **count** is less than or equal to 3, the statements within the braces of **for** are executed again.
- The body of the **for** loop continues to get executed till **count** does not exceed the final value 3.
- When **count** reaches the value 4, the control exits from the loop and is transferred to the statement (if any) immediately after the body of **for**.

The break Statement

We often come across situations where we want to jump out of a loop instantly, without waiting to get back to the conditional test. The keyword **break** allows us to do this. When **break** is encountered inside any loop, control automatically passes to the first statement after the loop. A **break** is usually associated with an **if**. As an example, let us consider Example 4.1.

Example 4.1: Write a program to determine whether a number is prime or not. A prime number is one, which is divisible only by 1 or itself.

All we have to do to test whether a number is prime or not, is to divide it successively by all numbers from 2 to one less than itself. If remainder of any of these divisions is zero, the number is not a prime. If no division yields a zero then the number is a prime number. Following program implements this logic.

```
# include <stdio.h>
int main( )
```

```
{
    int num, i ;

    printf ( "Enter a number " ) ;
    scanf ( "%d", &num ) ;

    i = 2 ;
    while ( i <= num - 1 )
    {
        if ( num % i == 0 )
        {
            printf ( "Not a prime number\n" ) ;
            break ;
        }
        i++ ;
    }

    if ( i == num )
        printf ( "Prime number\n" ) ;
}
```

In this program, the moment **num % i** turns out to be zero, (i.e. **num** is exactly divisible by **i**), the message "Not a prime number" is printed and the control breaks out of the **while** loop. Why does the program require the **if** statement after the **while** loop at all? Well, there are two ways the control could have reached outside the **while** loop:

(a) It jumped out because the number proved to be not a prime.
(b) The loop came to an end because the value of **i** became equal to **num**.

When the loop terminates in the second case, it means that there was no number between 2 to **num - 1** that could exactly divide **num**. That is, **num** is indeed a prime. If this is true, the program should print out the message "Prime number".

The continue Statement

In some programming situations, we want to take the control to the beginning of the loop, bypassing the statements inside the loop, which have not yet been executed. The keyword **continue** allows us to do this. When **continue** is encountered inside any loop, control automatically passes to the beginning of the loop.

A **continue** is usually associated with an **if**. As an example, let's consider the following program:

```
# include <stdio.h>
int main( )
{
    int  i, j ;

    for ( i = 1 ; i <= 2 ; i++ )
    {
        for ( j = 1 ; j <= 2 ; j++ )
        {
            if ( i == j )
                continue ;

            printf ( "% d % d\n", i, j ) ;
        }
    }
    return 0 ;
}
```

The output of the above program would be...

1 2
2 1

Note that when the value of **i** equals that of **j**, the **continue** statement takes the control to the **for** loop (inner) bypassing the rest of the statements pending execution in the **for** loop (inner).

The do-while Loop

The **do-while** loop looks like this:

```
do
{
    this ;
    and this ;
    and this ;
    and this ;
} while ( this condition is true ) ;
```

There is a minor difference between the working of **while** and **do-while** loops. This difference is the place where the condition is tested. The **while** tests the condition before executing any of the statements within the **while** loop. As against this, the **do-while** tests

Chapter 4: Loop Control Instruction

the condition after having executed the statements within the loop. This means that **do-while** would execute its statements at least once, even if the condition fails for the first time. The **while**, on the other hand will not execute its statements if the condition fails for the first time. Do not forget to place the semicolon at the end of **do-while** statement. This difference is brought about more clearly by the following program.

```
# include <stdio.h>
int main( )
{
    while ( 4 < 1 )
        printf ( "Hello there \n" ) ;
    return 0 ;
}
```

Here, since the condition fails the first time itself, the **printf( )** will not get executed at all. Let's now write the same program using a **do-while** loop.

```
# include <stdio.h>
int main( )
{
    do
    {
        printf ( "Hello there \n" ) ;
    } while ( 4 < 1 ) ;

    return 0 ;
}
```

In this program, the **printf( )** would be executed once, since first the body of the loop is executed and then the condition is tested.

ample Programs

(a) Write a program to calculate overtime pay of 10 employees. Overtime is paid at the rate of ₹ 12.00 per hour for every hour worked above 40 hours. Assume that employees do not work for fractional part of an hour.

Program:

```
/* Determine overtime pay of 10 employees.*/
# include <stdio.h>
int main( )
```

```c
    {
        float otpay ;
        int hour, i = 1 ;

        while ( i <= 10 )  /* Loop for 10 employees */
        {
            printf ( "\nEnter no. of hours worked: " ) ;
            scanf ( "%d", &hour ) ;

            if ( hour >= 40 )
            {
                otpay = ( hour - 40 ) * 12 ;
                printf ( "No of hours worked = %d \n
                        Overtime pay = Rs.%f\n", hour, otpay ) ;
            }
            else
            {
                otpay = 0 ;
                printf ( "No of hours worked (%d) is less than
                        40 Hrs.\nHence no overtime pay\n", hour ) ;
            }
            i++ ;
        }

        return 0 ;
    }
```

(b) Two numbers are entered through the keyboard. Write a program to find the value of one number raised to the power of another.

Program:

```c
/* Compute value of one number raised to another */
# include <stdio.h>
int main( )
{
    int x, y, i = 1 ;
    long int power = 1 ;

    printf ( "\nEnter two numbers: " ) ;
    scanf ( "%d %d", &x, &y ) ;

    while ( i <= y )
```

```
        {
            power = power * x ;
            i++ ;
        }
        printf ( "%d to the power %d is %ld\n", x, y, power ) ;

        return 0 ;
    }
```

(c) Ramanujan number is the smallest number that can be expressed as sum of two cubes in two different ways. Write a program to print all such numbers up to a reasonable limit.

Program:

```
/* Generate Ramanujan numbers */
#include <stdio.h>

int main( )
{
    int i, j, k, l ;

    for ( i = 1 ; i <= 30 ; i++ )
    {
        for ( j = 1 ; j <= 30 ; j++ )
        {
            for ( k = 1 ; k <= 30 ; k++ )
            {
                for ( l = 1 ; l <= 30 ; l++ )
                {
                    if ( ( ( i != j && i != k && i != l ) &&
                           ( j != i && j != k && j != l ) &&
                           ( k != i && k != j && k != l ) &&
                           ( l != i && l != j && l != k ) )
                    {
                        if ( i * i * i + j * j * j == k * k * k + l * l * l )
                            printf ( "%d %d %d %d\n", i, j, k, l ) ;
                    }
                }
            }
        }
    }
```

```
    return 0 ;
}
```

(d) Write a program to print 24 hours of day with suitable suffixes like AM, PM, Noon and Midnight.

Program:

```
/* Print hours of the day with suitable suffixes */
#include <stdio.h>

int main( )
{
    int hour ;

    for ( hour = 0 ; hour <= 23 ; hour++ )
    {
        if ( hour == 0 )
        {
            printf ( "12 Midnight\n" ) ;
            continue ;
        }

        if ( hour < 12 )
            printf ( "%d AM\n", hour ) ;

        if ( hour == 12 )
            printf ( "12 Noon\n" ) ;

        if ( hour > 12 )
            printf ( "%d PM\n", hour % 12 ) ;

    }
    return 0 ;
}
```

Chapter 4: Loop Control Instruction

Things to Remember

(a) The three type of loops available in C are **for**, **while**, and **do-while**.

(b) A **break** statement takes the execution control out of the loop.

(c) A **continue** statement skips the execution of the statements after it and takes the control through the next cycle of the loop.

(d) A **do-while** loop is used to ensure that the statements within the loop are executed at least once.

Exercise

[A] Answer the following:

(a) The three parts of the loop expression in the **for** loop are:

the i_____ expression
the t_____ expression
the i_____ expression

(b) The **break** statement is used to exit from:

1. an **if** statement
2. a **for** loop
3. a program
4. the **main( )** function

(c) A **do-while** loop is useful when we want that the statements within the loop must be executed:

1. Only once
2. At least once
3. More than once
4. None of the above

(d) In what sequence the initialization, testing and execution of body is done in a **do-while** loop

1. Initialization, execution of body, testing
2. Execution of body, initialization, testing
3. Initialization, testing, execution of body
4. None of the above

(e) Which of the following is not an infinite loop?

1. int i = 1 ;
   while (1)
   {
2. for (; ;) ;

3.  ```
    int t = 0, f ;
    while ( t )
    {
        f = 1 ;
    }
    ```

4.  ```
    int y, x = 0 ;
    do
    {
        y = x ;
    } while ( x == 0 ) ;
    ```

(f) Which keyword is used to take the control to the beginning of the loop?

[B] Attempt the following:

(a) Write a program to enter numbers till the user wants. At the end it should display the count of positive, negative and zeros entered.

(b) Write a program to find the range of a set of numbers entered through the keyboard. Range is the difference between the smallest and biggest number in the list.

(c) Write a program to print out all Armstrong numbers between 1 and 500. If sum of cubes of each digit of the number is equal to the number itself, then the number is called an Armstrong number. For example, 153 = (1 * 1 * 1) + (5 * 5 * 5) + (3 * 3 * 3).

(d) Write a program for a matchstick game being played between the computer and a user. Your program should ensure that the computer always wins. Rules for the game are as follows:

- There are 21 matchsticks.
- The computer asks the player to pick 1, 2, 3, or 4 matchsticks.
- After the person picks, the computer does its picking.
- Whoever is forced to pick up the last matchstick loses the game.

5 Functions

- What is a Function?
- Passing Values between Functions
- Sample Programs
- Things to Remember
- Sample Programs
- Exercise

Knowingly or unknowingly we rely on so many persons for so many things. Man is an intelligent species, but still cannot perform all of life's tasks all alone. He has to rely on others. You may call a mechanic to fix up your bike, hire a gardener to mow your lawn, or rely on a store to supply you groceries every month. A computer program (except for the simplest one) finds itself in a similar situation. It cannot handle all the tasks by itself. Instead, it requests other program-like entities—called 'functions' in C—to get its tasks done. In this Chapter we will study these functions. We will look at a variety of features of these functions, starting with the simplest one and then working towards those that demonstrate the power of C functions.

What is a Function?

A function is a self-contained block of statements that perform a coherent task of some kind. Every C program can be thought of as a collection of these functions. As we noted earlier, using a function is something like hiring a person to do a specific job for you. Sometimes the interaction with this person is very simple; sometimes it is complex.

Suppose you have a task that is always performed exactly in the same way—say a bimonthly servicing of your motorbike. When you want it to be done, you go to the service station and say, "It's time, do it now". You do not need to give instructions, because the mechanic knows his job. You do not need to be told how the job is done. You assume the bike would be serviced in the usual way, the mechanic does it and that's that.

Let us now look at a simple C function that operates in much the same way as the mechanic. Actually, we will be looking at two things—a function that calls or activates the function and the function itself.

```
# include <stdio.h>
void message( ) ;  /* function prototype declaration */
int main( )
{
    message( ) ;  /* function call */
    printf ( "Cry, and you stop the monotony!\n" ) ;
    return 0 ;
}
void message( )  /* function definition */
{
    printf ( "Smile, and the world smiles with you...\n" ) ;
}
```

The output of the above program when executed would be as follows:

Smile, and the world smiles with you...
Cry, and you stop the monotony!

Here, we have defined two functions—**main( )** and **message( )**. In fact we have used the word **message** at three places in the program. Let us understand the meaning of each.

The first is the function prototype and is written as:

void message( ) ;

This prototype declaration indicates that **message( )** is a function which after completing its execution does not return anything. This 'does not return anything' is indicated using the keyword **void**. It is necessary to mention the prototype of every function that we intend to define in the program.

The second usage of **message** is:

```
void message( )
{
    printf ( "Smile, and the world smiles with you...\n" ) ;
}
```

This is the function definition. In this definition right now we are having only **printf( )**, but we can also use **if, for, while, switch**, etc., within this function definition.

The third usage is:

message( ) ;

Here the function **message( )** is being called by **main( )**. What do we mean when we say that **main( )** 'calls' the function **message( )**? We mean that the control passes to the function **message( )**. The activity of **main( )** is temporarily suspended; it falls asleep while the **message( )** function wakes up and goes to work. When the **message( )** function runs out of statements to execute, the control returns to **main( )**, which comes to life again and begins executing its code at the exact point where it left off. Thus, **main( )** becomes the 'calling' function, whereas **message( )** becomes the 'called' function.

If you have grasped the concept of 'calling' a function you are prepared for a call to more than one function. Consider the following example:

```
# include <stdio.h>
void italy( ) ;
```

```c
void brazil( ) ;
void argentina( ) ;
int main( )
{
    printf ( "I am in main\n" ) ;
    italy( ) ;
    brazil( ) ;
    argentina( ) ;
    return 0 ;
}
void italy( )
{
    printf ( "I am in italy\n" ) ;
}
void brazil( )
{
    printf ( "I am in brazil\n" ) ;
}
void argentina( )
{
    printf ( "I am in argentina\n" ) ;
}
```

The output of the above program when executed would be as follows:

I am in main
I am in italy
I am in brazil
I am in argentina

A number of conclusions can be drawn from this program:

- A C program is a collection of one or more functions.

- If a C program contains only one function, it must be **main( )**.

- If a C program contains more than one function, then one (and only one) of these functions must be **main( )**, because program execution always begins with **main( )**.

- There is no limit on the number of functions that might be present in a C program.

- Each function in a program is called in the sequence specified by the function calls in **main( )**.

Chapter 5: Functions

- After each function has done its thing, control returns to **main( )**. When **main( )** runs out of statements and function calls, the program ends.

As we have noted earlier, the program execution always begins with **main( )**. Except for this fact, all C functions enjoy a state of perfect equality. No precedence, no priorities, nobody is nobody's boss. One function can call another function it has already called but has in the meantime left temporarily in order to call a third function which will sometime later call the function that has called it, if you understand what I mean. No? Well, let's illustrate with an example.

```c
# include <stdio.h>
void italy( ) ;
void brazil( ) ;
void argentina( ) ;
int main( )
{
    printf ( "I am in main\n" ) ;
    italy( ) ;
    printf ( "I am finally back in main\n" ) ;
    return 0 ;
}
void italy( )
{
    printf ( "I am in italy\n" ) ;
    brazil( ) ;
    printf ( "I am back in italy\n" ) ;
}
void brazil( )
{
    printf ( "I am in brazil\n" ) ;
    argentina( ) ;
}
void argentina( )
{
    printf ( "I am in argentina\n" ) ;
}
```

The output of the above program when executed would be as follows:

```
I am in main
I am in italy
I am in brazil
I am in argentina
```

I am back in italy
I am finally back in main

Here, **main( )** calls other functions, which in turn call still other functions. Trace carefully the way control passes from one function to another. Since the compiler always begins the program execution with **main( )**, every function in a program must be called directly or indirectly by **main( )**. In other words, the **main( )** function drives other functions.

Let us now summarize what we have learnt so far.

(a) A function gets called when the function name is followed by a semicolon (;). For example,

```
int main( )
{
    argentina( ) ;
}
```

(b) A function is defined when function name is followed by a pair of braces in which one or more statements may be present. For example,

```
void argentina( )
{
    statement 1 ;
    statement 2 ;
    statement 3 ;
}
```

(c) Any function can be called from any other function. Even **main( )** can be called from other functions. For example,

```
# include <stdio.h>
void message( ) ;
int main( )
{
    message( ) ;
    return 0 ;
}
void message( )
{
    printf ( "Can't imagine life without C\n" ) ;
    main( ) ;
```

}

(d) A function can be called any number of times. For example,

```
# include <stdio.h>
void message( ) ;
int main( )
{
    message( ) ;
    message( ) ;
    return 0 ;
}
void message( )
{
    printf ( "Jewel Thief!!\n" ) ;
}
```

(e) The order in which the functions are defined in a program and the order in which they get called need not necessarily be same. For example,

```
# include <stdio.h>
void message1( ) ;
void message2( ) ;
int main( )
{
    message1( ) ;
    message2( ) ;
    return 0 ;
}
void message2( )
{
    printf ( "But the butter was bitter\n" ) ;
}
void message1( )
{
    printf ( "Mary bought some butter\n" ) ;
}
```

Here, even though **message1( )** is getting called before **message2( )**, still, **message1( )** has been defined after **message2( )**. However, it is advisable to define the functions in the same order in which they are called. This makes the program easier to understand.

(f) A function can call itself. Such a process is called 'recursion'. We would discuss this aspect of C functions later in this chapter.

(g) A function can be called from another function, but a function cannot be defined in another function. Thus, the following program code would be wrong, since **argentina( )** is being defined inside another function, **main( )**.

```
int main( )
{
    printf ( "I am in main\n" ) ;
    void argentina( )
    {
        printf ( "I am in argentina\n" ) ;
    }
}
```

(h) There are basically two types of functions:

Library functions, for example **printf( )**, **scanf( )**, etc.
User-defined functions, for example, **argentina( )**, **brazil( )**, etc.

As the name suggests, library functions are commonly required functions grouped together and stored in a Library. This library of functions is present on the disk and is written for us by people who write compilers for us. Almost always, a compiler comes with a library of standard functions. The procedure of calling both types of functions is exactly same.

Passing Values between Functions

The functions that we have used so far have not been very flexible. We call them and they do what they are designed to do. Like our mechanic who always services the motorbike in exactly the same way, we have not been able to influence the functions in the way they carry out their tasks. It would be nice to have a little more control over what functions do, in the same way it would be nice to be able to tell the mechanic, "Also change the engine oil, I am going for an outing". In short, now we want to communicate between the 'calling' and the 'called' functions.

The mechanism used to convey information to the function is the 'argument'. You have unknowingly used the arguments in the **printf( )** and **scanf( )** functions; the format string and the list of variables used inside the parentheses in these functions are arguments. The arguments are sometimes also called 'parameters'.

Chapter 5: Functions

Consider the following program. In this program, in **main( )** we receive the values of **a, b** and **c** through the keyboard and then output the sum of **a, b** and **c**. However, the calculation of sum is done in a different function called **calsum( )**. If sum is to be calculated in **calsum( )** and values of **a, b** and **c** are received in **main( )**, then we must pass on these values to **calsum( )**, and once **calsum( )** calculates the sum, we must return it from **calsum( )** back to **main( )**.

```
/* Sending and receiving values between functions */
# include <stdio.h>
int calsum ( int x, int y, int z ) ;
int main( )
{
    int a, b, c, sum ;
    printf ( "Enter any three numbers " ) ;
    scanf ( "%d %d %d", &a, &b, &c ) ;
    sum = calsum ( a, b, c ) ;
    printf ( "Sum = %d\n", sum ) ;
    return 0 ;
}
int calsum ( int x, int y, int z )
{
    int d ;

    d = x + y + z ;
    return ( d ) ;
}
```

The output of the above program when executed would be as follows:

Enter any three numbers 10 20 30
Sum = 60

There are a number of things to note about this program:

(a) In this program, from the function **main( )**, the values of **a, b** and **c** are passed on to the function **calsum( )**, by making a call to the function **calsum( )** and mentioning **a, b** and **c** in the parentheses:

sum = calsum (a, b, c) ;

In the **calsum( )** function, these values get collected in three variables **x, y** and **z**:

```
int calsum ( int x, int y, int z )
```

(b) The variables **a**, **b** and **c** are called 'actual arguments', whereas the variables **x**, **y** and **z** are called 'formal arguments'. Any number of arguments can be passed to a function being called. However, the type, order and number of the actual and formal arguments must always be same.

Instead of using different variable names **x**, **y** and **z**, we could have used the same variable names **a**, **b** and **c**. But the compiler would still treat them as different variables since they are in different functions.

(c) Note the function prototype declaration of **calsum( )**. Instead of the usual **void**, we are using **int**. This indicates that **calsum( )** is going to return a value of the type **int**. It is not compulsory to use variable names in the prototype declaration. Hence we could as well have written the prototype as:

```
int calsum ( int, int, int ) ;
```

In the definition of **calsum** too, **void** has been replaced by **int**.

(d) In the earlier programs, the moment closing brace (}) of the called function was encountered, the control returned to the calling function. No separate **return** statement was necessary to send back the control.

This approach is fine if the called function is not going to return any meaningful value to the calling function. In the above program, however, we want to return the sum of **x**, **y** and **z**. Therefore, it is necessary to use the **return** statement.

The **return** statement serves two purposes:

(1) On executing the **return** statement, it immediately transfers the control back to the calling function.
(2) It returns the value present in the parentheses after **return**, to the calling function. In the above program, the value of sum of three numbers is being returned.

(e) There is no restriction on the number of **return** statements that may be present in a function. Also, the **return** statement need not always be present at the end of the called function. The following program illustrates these facts:

```
int fun( )
{
    int n ;
```

Chapter 5: Functions

```
        printf ( "Enter any number " ) ;
        scanf ( "%d", &n ) ;
        if ( n >= 10 && n <= 90 )
            return ( n ) ;
        else
            return ( n + 32 ) ;
    }
```

In this function, different **return** statements will be executed depending on whether **n** is between 10 and 90.

(f) Whenever the control returns from a function, the sum being returned is collected in the calling function by equating the called function to some variable. For example,

sum = calsum (a, b, c) ;

(g) All the following are valid **return** statements.

return (a) ;
return (23) ;
return ;

In the last statement, a garbage value is returned to the calling function since we are not returning any specific value. Note that, in this case, the parentheses after **return** are dropped. In the other **return** statements too, the parentheses can be dropped.

(h) A function can return only one value at a time. Thus, the following statements are invalid.

return (a, b) ;
return (x, 12) ;

(i) If the value of a formal argument is changed in the called function, the corresponding change does not take place in the calling function. For example,

```
# include <stdio.h>
void fun ( int ) ;
int main( )
{
    int a = 30 ;
    fun ( a ) ;
    printf ( "%d\n", a ) ;
```

```
        return 0 ;
}
void fun ( int b )
{
    b = 60 ;
    printf ( "%d\n", b ) ;
}
```

The output of the above program when executed would be as follows:

```
60
30
```

Thus, even though the value of **b** is changed in **fun( )**, the value of **a** in **main( )** remains unchanged. This means that when values are passed to a called function, the values present in actual arguments are not physically moved to the formal arguments; just a photocopy of values in actual argument is made into formal arguments.

Sample Programs

(a) Write a function that receives marks received by a student in 3 subjects and returns the average marks. Call this function from **main( )** and print the results in **main( )**.

Program:

```
/* Function which returns average and percentage */
# include <stdio.h>

int result ( int, int, int ) ;
int main( )
{
    float avg ;
    int m1, m2, m3 ;

    printf ( "Enter marks of three subjects: " ) ;
    scanf ( "%d %d %d", &m1, &m2, &m3 ) ;
    avg = result ( m1, m2, m3 ) ;
    printf ( "Average = %f \n", avg ) ;

    return 0 ;
}
```

```c
int result ( int m1, int m2, int m3 )
{
    int a ;
    a = ( m1 + m2 + m3 ) / 3 ;
    return a ;
}
```

(b) A 5-digit positive integer is entered through the keyboard, write a function to calculate sum of digits of the 5-digit number.

Program:

```c
/* Calculate sum of digits of a five-digit number with/without recursion */
# include <stdio.h>

int sum ( int ) ;  /* Function without recursion */
int main( )
{
    int s, n ;

    printf ( "Enter number" ) ;
    scanf ( "% d", &n ) ;

    s = sum ( n ) ;
    printf ( "Sum of digits = % d\n", s ) ;

    return 0 ;
}
int sum ( int num )
{
    int remainder, sum = 0 ;

    while ( num > 0 )
    {
        remainder = num % 10 ;  /* Calculate remainder */
        sum = sum + remainder ;  /* update sum */
        num = num / 10 ;  /* Remove last digit */
    }

    return ( sum ) ;
}
```

(c) If the lengths of the sides of a triangle are denoted by **a**, **b**, and **c**, then area of triangle is given by:

$$area = \sqrt{S(S-a)(S-b)(S-c)}$$

where, S = (a + b + c) / 2. Write a function to calculate the area of the triangle.

Program:

```
/* Area of triangle with sides a, b & c */
# include <stdio.h>
# include <math.h>

float area ( float a, float b, float c ) ;
int main( )
{
    float a, b, c, z ;

    printf ( "\nEnter three sides of the triangle: " ) ;
    scanf ( "%f%f%f", &a, &b, &c ) ;
    z = area ( a, b, c ) ;
    printf ( "\n\nArea of the triangle = %.3f\n", z ) ;
    return 0 ;
}

/* Function to calculate area from a formula */
float area ( float a, float b, float c )
{
    float s, m, x ;
    s = ( a + b + c ) / 2 ;
    m = s * ( s - a ) * ( s - b ) * ( s - c ) ;
    x = sqrt ( m ) ;

    return ( x ) ;
}
```

Things to Remember

(a) To avoid repetition of code and bulky programs functionally related statements are isolated into a function.

Chapter 5: Functions

(b) Function declaration specifies the return type of the function and the types of parameters it accepts.

(c) Function definition defines the body of the function.

(d) Variables declared in a function are not available to other functions in a program. So, there will not be any clash even if we give same name to the variables declared in different functions.

(e) Adding too many functions and calling them frequently may slow down the program execution.

Exercise

[A] State whether the following statements are True or False:

(a) The variables commonly used in C functions are available to all the functions in a program.

(b) To return the control back to the calling function we must use the keyword **return**.

(c) The same variable names can be used in different functions without any conflict.

(d) Every called function must contain a **return** statement.

(e) A function may contain more than one **return** statement.

(f) Each **return** statement in a function may return a different value.

(g) A function can still be useful even if you do not pass any arguments to it and the function does not return any value back.

(h) Same names can be used for different functions without any conflict.

(i) A function may be called more than once from any other function.

(j) It is necessary for a function to return some value.

(k) If the function is not going to return any value to the calling function then the return type of the function must be **void**.

[B] Attempt the following:

(a) Write a function **power (a, b)**, to calculate the value of **a** raised to **b**.

(b) Write a general-purpose function to convert any given year into its roman equivalent. Use these roman equivalents for decimal numbers: 1 – I, 5 – V, 10 – X, 50 – L, 100 – C, 500 – D, 1000 – M.

Example:

Roman equivalent of 1988 is mdccclxxxviii
Roman equivalent of 1525 is mdxxv

(c) Any year is entered through the keyboard. Write a function to determine whether the year is a leap year or not.

6 Arrays

- What is C?
- What are Arrays?
    - A Simple Program using Array
- More on Arrays
    - Arrays Initialization
    - Bounds Checking
    - Passing Array Elements to a Function
- Two-Dimensional Arrays
    - Initializing a Two-Dimensional Array
- Sample Programs
- Things to Remember
- Exercise

C language provides a capability that enables the user to design a set of similar data types, called array. The elements of an array are arranged systematically in memory and they can be accessed using their position in the array. This Chapter describes how arrays can be created and manipulated in C.

What are Arrays?

For understanding the arrays properly, let us consider the following program:

```
# include <stdio.h>
int main( )
{
    int x ;
    x = 5 ;
    x = 10 ;
    printf ( "x = %d\n", x ) ;
    return 0 ;
}
```

No doubt, this program will print the value of **x** as 10. Why so? Because, when a value 10 is assigned to **x**, the earlier value of **x**, i.e. 5, is lost. Thus, ordinary variables (the ones which we have used so far) are capable of holding only one value at a time (as in this example). However, there are situations in which we would want to store more than one value at a time in a single variable.

For example, suppose we wish to arrange the percentage marks obtained by 100 students in ascending order. In such a case, we have two options to store these marks in memory:

(a) Construct 100 variables to store percentage marks obtained by 100 different students, i.e., each variable containing one student's marks.

(b) Construct one variable (called array or subscripted variable) capable of storing or holding all the hundred values.

Obviously, the second alternative is better. A simple reason for this is, it would be much easier to handle one variable than handling 100 different variables. Moreover, there are certain logics that cannot be dealt with, without the use of an array. Now a formal definition of an array—An array is a collective name given to a group of 'similar quantities'. These similar quantities could be percentage marks of 100 students, or salaries of 300 employees, or ages of 50 employees. What is important is that the quantities must be 'similar'. Each member in the group is referred to by its position in the group. For example, assume the following group of numbers, which represent percentage marks obtained by five students.

Chapter 6: Arrays

per = { 48, 88, 34, 23, 96 }

If we want to refer to the second number of the group, the usual notation used is per_2. Similarly, the fourth number of the group is referred as per_4. However, in C, the fourth number is referred as **per[3]**. This is because, in C, the counting of elements begins with 0 and not with 1. Thus, in this example **per[3]** refers to 23 and **per[4]** refers to 96. In general, the notation would be **per[i]**, where, **i** can take a value 0, 1, 2, 3, or 4, depending on the position of the element being referred. Here **per** is the subscripted variable (array), whereas **i** is its subscript.

Thus, an array is a collection of similar elements. These similar elements could be all **int**s, or all **float**s, or all **char**s, etc. Usually, the array of characters is called a 'string', whereas an array of **int**s or **float**s is called simply an array. Remember that all elements of any given array must be of the same type. i.e., we cannot have an array of 10 numbers, of which 5 are **int**s and 5 are **float**s.

A Simple Program using Array

Let us try to write a program to find average marks obtained by a class of 30 students in a test.

```c
# include <stdio.h>
int main( )
{
    int  avg, sum = 0 ;
    int  i ;
    int  marks[ 30 ] ;  /* array declaration */

    for ( i = 0 ; i <= 29 ; i++ )
    {
        printf ( "Enter marks " ) ;
        scanf ( "%d", &marks[ i ] ) ;  /* store data in array */
    }

    for ( i = 0 ; i <= 29 ; i++ )
        sum = sum + marks[ i ] ;  /* read data from an array*/

    avg = sum / 30 ;
    printf ( "Average marks = %d\n", avg ) ;
    return 0 ;
}
```

There is a lot of new material in this program, so let us take it apart slowly.

Array Declaration

To begin with, like other variables, an array needs to be declared so that the compiler will know what kind of an array and how large an array we want. In our program, we have done this with the statement:

int marks[30] ;

Here, **int** specifies the type of the variable, just as it does with ordinary variables and the word **marks** specifies the name of the variable. The **[30]** however is new. The number 30 tells how many elements of the type **int** will be in our array. This number is often called the 'dimension' of the array. The brackets ([ ]) tells the compiler that we are dealing with an array.

Accessing Elements of an Array

Once an array is declared, let us see how individual elements in the array can be referred. This is done with subscript, the number in the brackets following the array name. This number specifies the element's position in the array. All the array elements are numbered, starting with 0. Thus, **marks[2]** is not the second element of the array, but the third. In our program, we are using the variable **i** as a subscript to refer to various elements of the array. This variable can take different values and hence can refer to the different elements in the array in turn. This ability to use variables to represent subscripts is what makes arrays so useful.

Entering Data into an Array

Here is the section of code that places data into an array:

```
for ( i = 0 ; i <= 29 ; i++ )
{
    printf ( "Enter marks " ) ;
    scanf ( "%d", &marks[ i ] ) ;
}
```

The **for** loop causes the process of asking for and receiving a student's marks from the user to be repeated 30 times. The first time through the loop, **i** has a value 0, so the **scanf( )** function will cause the value typed to be stored in the array element **marks[0]**, the first element of the array. This process will be repeated until **i** becomes 29. This is last

Chapter 6: Arrays

time through the loop, which is a good thing, because there is no array element like **marks[30]**.

In **scanf( )** function, we have used the "address of" operator (&) on the element **marks[i]** of the array, just as we have used it earlier on other variables (**&rate**, for example). In doing so, we are passing the address of this particular array element to the **scanf( )** function, rather than its value; which is what **scanf( )** requires.

Reading Data from an Array

The balance of the program reads the data back out of the array and uses it to calculate the average. The **for** loop is much the same, but now the body of the loop causes each student's marks to be added to a running total stored in a variable called **sum**. When all the marks have been added up, the result is divided by 30, the number of students, to get the average.

```
for ( i = 0 ; i <= 29 ; i++ )
    sum = sum + marks[ i ] ;

avg = sum / 30 ;
printf ( "Average marks = % d\n", avg ) ;
```

To fix our ideas, let us revise whatever we have learnt about arrays:

(a) An array is a collection of similar elements.
(b) The first element in the array is numbered 0, so the last element is 1 less than the size of the array.
(c) An array is also known as a subscripted variable.
(d) Before using an array, its type and dimension must be declared.
(e) However big an array, its elements are always stored in contiguous memory locations. This is a very important point which we would discuss in more detail later on.

More on Arrays

Array is a very popular data type with C programmers. This is because of the convenience with which arrays lend themselves to programming. The features which make arrays so convenient to program would be discussed below, along with the possible pitfalls in using them.

Array Initialization

So far we have used arrays that did not have any values in them to begin with. We managed to store values in them during program execution. Let us now see how to initialize an array while declaring it. Following are a few examples that demonstrate this:

```
int num[ 6 ] = { 2, 4, 12, 5, 45, 5 } ;
int n[ ] = { 2, 4, 12, 5, 45, 5 } ;
float press[ ] = { 12.3, 34.2, -23.4, -11.3 } ;
```

Note the following points carefully:

(a) Till the array elements are not given any specific values, they are supposed to contain garbage values.

(b) If the array is initialized where it is declared, mentioning the dimension of the array is optional as in the 2nd and 3rd example above.

Bounds Checking

In C, there is no check to see if the subscript used for an array exceeds the size of the array. Data entered with a subscript exceeding the array size will simply be placed in memory outside the array; probably on top of other data, or on the program itself. This will lead to unpredictable results, to say the least, and there will be no error message to warn you that you are going beyond the array size. In some cases, the computer may just hang. Thus, the behavior of the following program may turn out to be unpredictable.

```
# include <stdio.h>
int main( )
{
    int num[ 40 ], i ;

    for ( i = 0 ; i <= 100 ; i++ )
        num[ i ] = i ;
    return 0 ;
}
```

Thus, to see to it that we do not reach beyond the array size, is entirely the programmer's botheration and not the compiler's.

Passing Array Elements to a Function

Array elements can be passed to a function as shown below.

```
/* Passing array elements to a function */
# include <stdio.h>
void display ( int ) ;
int main( )
{
    int i ;
    int marks[ ] = { 55, 65, 75, 56, 78, 78, 90 } ;
    for ( i = 0 ; i <= 6 ; i++ )
        display ( marks[ i ] ) ;
    return 0 ;
}
void display ( int m )
{
    printf ( "%d ", m ) ;
}
```

The output of the above program when executed would be as follows:

55 65 75 56 78 78 90

Here, we are passing an individual array element at a time to the function **display( )** and getting it printed in the function **display( )**. Note that, since at a time only one element is being passed, this element is collected in an ordinary integer variable **m**, in the function **display( )**.

Two-Dimensional Arrays

So far, we have explored arrays with only one dimension. It is also possible for arrays to have two or more dimensions. The two-dimensional array is also called a matrix.

Here is a sample program that stores roll number and marks obtained by a student side by side in a matrix.

```
# include <stdio.h>
int main( )
{
    int stud[ 4 ][ 2 ] ;
    int i, j ;
```

```
    for ( i = 0 ; i <= 3 ; i++ )
    {
        printf ( "Enter roll no. and marks" ) ;
        scanf ( "% d % d", &stud[ i ][ 0 ], &stud[ i ][ 1 ] ) ;
    }
    for ( i = 0 ; i <= 3 ; i++ )
        printf ( "% d % d\n", stud[ i ][ 0 ], stud[ i ][ 1 ] ) ;
    return 0 ;
}
```

There are two parts to the program—in the first part, through a **for** loop, we read in the values of roll no. and marks, whereas, in the second part through another **for** loop, we print out these values.

Look at the **scanf( )** statement used in the first **for** loop:

scanf ("% d % d", &stud[i][0], &stud[i][1]) ;

In **stud[i][0]** and **stud[i][1]**, the first subscript of the variable **stud**, is row number which changes for every student. The second subscript tells which of the two columns are we talking about—the zeroth column which contains the roll no. or the first column which contains the marks. Remember the counting of rows and columns begin with zero. The complete array arrangement is shown in Figure 6.1.

	col. no. 0	col. no. 1
row no. 0	1234	56
row no. 1	1212	33
row no. 2	1434	80
row no. 3	1312	78

Figure 6.1 Elements arranged in Two-Dimensional Array

Thus, 1234 is stored in **stud[0][0]**, 56 is stored in **stud[0][1]** and so on (Refer Figure 6.1). The above arrangement highlights the fact that a two-dimensional array is a collection of a number of one-dimensional arrays placed one below the other.

In our sample program, the array elements have been stored row-wise and accessed row-wise. However, you can access the array elements column-wise as well. Traditionally, the array elements are being stored and accessed row-wise; therefore we would also stick to the same strategy.

Initializing a Two-Dimensional Array

How do we initialize a two-dimensional array? As simple as this:

```
int  stud[ 4 ][ 2 ] = {
                { 1234, 56 },
                { 1212, 33 },
                { 1434, 80 },
                { 1312, 78 }
              } ;
```

or even this would work...

int stud[4][2] = { 1234, 56, 1212, 33, 1434, 80, 1312, 78 } ;

of course, with a corresponding loss in readability.

It is important to remember that, while initializing a 2-D array, it is necessary to mention the second (column) dimension, whereas the first dimension (row) is optional.

Thus the declarations,

int arr[2][3] = { 12, 34, 23, 45, 56, 45 } ;
int arr[ ][3] = { 12, 34, 23, 45, 56, 45 } ;

are perfectly acceptable,

whereas,

int arr[2][ ] = { 12, 34, 23, 45, 56, 45 } ;
int arr[ ][ ] = { 12, 34, 23, 45, 56, 45 } ;

would never work.

Sample Programs

(a) Twenty-five numbers are entered from the keyboard into an array. Write a program to find out how many of them are positive, how many are negative, how many are even and how many odd.

Program

```c
/* Program to count positive, negative, odd & even nos in an array */
# include <stdio.h>

int main( )
{
    int  num[ 25 ], i, neg = 0, pos = 0, odd = 0, even = 0 ;

    printf ( "Enter 25 elements of array" ) ;
    for ( i = 0 ; i <= 24 ; i++ )
        scanf ( "% d", &num[ i ] ) ;  /* Array Elements */

    for ( i = 0 ; i <= 24 ; i++ )
    {
        if ( num[ i ] < 0 )
            neg++ ;
        else
            pos++ ;

        if ( num[ i ] % 2 == 0 )
            even++ ;
        else
            odd++ ;
    }

    printf ( "Negative elements = % d\n", neg ) ;
    printf ( "Positive elements = % d\n", pos ) ;
    printf ( "Even elements = % d\n", even ) ;
    printf ( "Odd elements = % d\n", odd ) ;

    return 0 ;
}
```

(b) Write a program that interchanges the elements in odd position with elements in even position in an array.

```
/* Program to exchange odd and even position elements in an array */
# include <stdio.h>

int main( )
{
    int  num[ ] = { 12, 4, 5, 1, 9, 13, 11, 19, 54, 34 } ;
    int i, t ;

    for ( i = 0 ; i <= 9 ; i = i + 2 )
    {
        t = num[ i ] ;
        num [ i ] = num [ i + 1 ] ;
        num [ i + 1 ] = t ;
    }

    for ( i = 0 ; i <= 9 ; i++ )
        printf ( "% d\n", num[ i ] ) ;

    return 0 ;
}
```

(c) Write a program to obtain transpose of a 4 x 4 matrix. The transpose of a matrix is obtained by exchanging the elements of each row with the elements of the corresponding column.

Program:

```
/* Transpose of a 4 x 4 matrix */
# include <stdio.h>

int main( )
{
    int  mat[ 4 ][ 4 ], i, j, temp ;

    printf ( "\nEnter values for 4 x 4 matrix:\n " ) ;

    for ( i = 0 ; i <= 3 ; i++ )
    {
        for ( j = 0 ; j <= 3 ; j++ )
```

```c
            scanf ( "%d", &mat[ i ][ j ] ) ;
    }

    printf ( "\n\nThe matrix you entered is:\n" ) ;

    for ( i = 0 ; i <= 3 ; i++ )
    {
        for ( j = 0 ; j <= 3 ; j++ )
            printf ( "%d\t", mat[ i ][ j ] ) ;

        printf ( "\n" ) ;
    }

    /* Transpose the matrix */
    for ( i = 0 ; i <= 3 ; i++ )
    {
        for ( j = i + 1 ; j <= 3 ; j++ )
        {
            temp = mat[ i ][ j ] ;
            mat[ i ][ j ] = mat[ j ][ i ] ;
            mat[ j ][ i ] = temp ;
        }
    }

    printf ( "\n\nTranspose of the matrix is:\n" ) ;
    for ( i = 0 ; i <= 3 ; i++ )
    {
        for ( j = 0 ; j <= 3 ; j++ )
            printf ( "%d\t", mat[ i ][ j ] ) ;
        printf ( "\n" ) ;
    }

    return 0 ;
}
```

Things to Remember

(a) An array is similar to an ordinary variable except that it can store multiple elements of similar type.

(b) Array elements are counted from 0 onwards.

(c) Compiler does not perform bounds checking on an array.

Chapter 6: Arrays

(d) Zeroth element is a single value, whereas, in a 2-D array this element is a 1-D array.

Exercise

[A] Answer the following:

(a) An array is a collection of:
  1. Different data types scattered throughout memory.
  2. The same data type scattered throughout memory.
  3. The same data type placed next to each other in memory.
  4. Different data types placed next to each other in memory.

(b) Are the following array declarations correct?
```
int a (25) ;
int size = 10, b[ size ] ;
int c = {0,1,2} ;
```

(c) Which element of the array does this expression reference?
```
num[ 4 ]
```

(d) What is the difference between the 5's in the following two expressions?
```
int num[ 5 ] ;
num[ 5 ] = 11 ;
```
  1. First is particular element, second is type.
  2. First is array size, second is particular element.
  3. First is particular element, second is array size.
  4. Both specify array size.

(e) State whether the following statements are True or False:
  1. The array **int num[26]** has twenty-six elements.
  2. The expression **num[1]** designates the first element in the array.
  3. It is necessary to initialize the array at the time of declaration.
  4. The expression **num[27]** designates the twenty-eighth element in the array.

(f) What will happen if you try to put so many values into an array when you initialize it that the size of the array is exceeded?
  1. Nothing.
  2. Possible system malfunction.
  3. Error message from the compiler.
  4. Other data may be overwritten.

(g) In an array **int arr[12]** the word **arr** represents the a_____ of the array.

(h) What will happen if you put too few elements in an array when you initialize it?
   1. Error message would be displayed during Compilation.
   2. An endless loop would be created while accessing the array.
   3. Buffer overflow.
   4. Unused elements will be filled with 0's or garbage.

(i) What will happen if you assign a value to an element of an array whose subscript exceeds the size of the array?
   1. The element will be set to 0.
   2. Nothing, it's done all the time.
   3. Other data may be overwritten.
   4. Error message from the compiler.

[B] Attempt the following:

(a) Write a program to pick up the largest number from any 5 row by 5 column matrix.

(b) Twenty-five numbers are entered from the keyboard into an array. The number to be searched is entered through the keyboard by the user. Write a program to find if the number to be searched is present in the array and if it is present, display the number of times it appears in the array.

(c) Write a program to obtain sum of all elements above the diagonal and below the diagonal elements of a 5 row by 5 column matrix.

7 Strings

- What are Strings?
- More about Strings
- Standard Library String Functions
- Two-Dimensional Array of Characters
- Sample Programs
- Things to Remember
- Exercise

In the last Chapter, you have learnt how to define arrays of various sizes and dimensions, how to initialize arrays, how to pass arrays to a function, etc. With this knowledge under your belt, you should be ready to handle strings, which are, simply put, a special kind of array. And strings and the ways to manipulate them are going to be the topics of discussion in this Chapter.

What are Strings?

The way a group of integers can be stored in an integer array, similarly a group of characters can be stored in a character array. Character arrays are many a time also called strings. Many languages internally treat strings as character arrays, but somehow conceal this fact from the programmer. Character arrays or strings are used by programming languages to manipulate text, such as words and sentences.

A string constant is a one-dimensional array of characters terminated by a null ('\0'). For example,

char name[ ] = { 'H', 'A', 'E', 'S', 'L', 'E', 'R', '\0' } ;

Each character in the array occupies one byte of memory and the last character is always '\0'. What character is this? It looks like two characters, but it is actually only one character, i.e. 0, with the \ indicating that what follows it is something special. '\0' is called null character. Note that '\0' and '0' are not same. ASCII value of '\0' is 0, whereas ASCII value of '0' is 48. The terminating null ('\0') is important, because it is the only way the functions that work with a string can know where the string ends. In fact, a string not terminated by a '\0' is not really a string, but merely a collection of characters.

C concedes the fact that you would use strings very often and hence provides a shortcut for initializing strings. For example, the string used above can also be initialized as,

char name[ ] = "HAESLER" ;

Note that, in this declaration '\0' is not necessary. C inserts the null character automatically.

More about Strings

In what way are character arrays different from numeric arrays? Can elements in a character array be accessed in the same way as the elements of a numeric array? Do I need to take any special care of '\0'? Why numeric arrays do not end with a '\0'?

Chapter 7: Strings

Declaring strings is okay, but how do I manipulate them? Questions galore!! Well, let us settle some of these issues right away with the help of sample programs.

```
/* Program to demonstrate printing of a string */
# include <stdio.h>
int main( )
{
    char  name[ ] = "Klinsman" ;
    int  i = 0 ;

    while ( i <= 7 )
    {
        printf ( "%c", name[ i ] ) ;
        i++ ;
    }
    printf ( "\n" ) ;
    return 0 ;
}
```

The output of the above program on execution would be as follows:

Klinsman

No big deal. We have initialized a character array, and then printed out the elements of this array within a **while** loop. Can we write the **while** loop without using the final value 7? We can; because we know that each character array always ends with a '\0'. Following program illustrates this:

```
# include <stdio.h>
int main( )
{
    char  name[ ] = "Klinsman" ;
    int  i = 0 ;
    while ( name[ i ] != '\0' )
    {
        printf ( "%c", name[ i ] ) ;
        i++ ;
    }
    printf ( "\n" ) ;
    return 0 ;
}
```

The output of the above program on execution would be as follows:

Klinsman

This program does not rely on the length of the string (number of characters in it) to print out its contents and hence is definitely more general than the earlier one.

Though there are different ways (as shown above) to refer to the elements of a character array, rarely is any one of them used. This is because **printf( )** function has got a sweet and simple way of doing it, as shown below. Note that **printf( )** does not print the '\0'.

```
# include <stdio.h>
int main( )
{
    char  name[ ] = "Klinsman" ;
    printf ( "%s", name ) ;
}
```

The **%s** used in **printf( )** is a format specification for printing out a string. The same specification can be used to receive a string from the keyboard, as shown below.

```
# include <stdio.h>
int main( )
{
    char  name[ 25 ] ;

    printf ( "Enter your name " ) ;
    scanf ( "%s", name ) ;
    printf ( "Hello %s!\n", name ) ;
    return 0 ;
}
```

The output of the above program on execution would be as follows:

Enter your name Debashish
Hello Debashish!

Note that the declaration **char name[25]** sets aside 25 bytes under the array **name[ ]**, whereas the **scanf( )** function fills in the characters typed at keyboard into this array until the Enter key is hit. Once enter is hit, **scanf( )** places a '\0' in the array.

Chapter 7: Strings

Standard Library String Functions

With every C compiler, a large set of useful string handling library functions are provided. Table 7.1 lists the more commonly used functions along with their purpose.

Function	Use
strlen	Finds length of a string.
strlwr	Converts a string to lowercase.
strupr	Converts a string to uppercase.
strcat	Appends one string at the end of another.
strncat	Appends first n characters of a string at the end of another.
strcpy	Copies a string into another.
strncpy	Copies first n characters of one string into another.
strcmp	Compares two strings.
strncmp	Compares first n characters of two strings.
strcmpi	Compares two strings without regard to case ("i" denotes that this function ignores case).
stricmp	Compares two strings without regard to case (identical to strcmpi).
strnicmp	Compares first n characters of two strings without regard to case.
strdup	Duplicates a string.
strchr	Finds first occurrence of a given character in a string.
strrchr	Finds last occurrence of a given character in a string.
strstr	Finds first occurrence of a given string in another string.
strset	Sets all characters of string to a given character.
strnset	Sets first n characters of a string to a given character.
strrev	Reverses string.

Table 7.1 String Functions

Out of the above list, we shall discuss the functions **strlen( )**, **strcpy( )**, **strcat( )** and **strcmp( )**, since these are the most commonly used functions. The following program shows how they can be used:

```
# include <stdio.h>
# include <string.h>
int main( )
{
    char  str[ ] = "Bamboozled" ;
    int  len ;
    char  source1[ ] = "Sayonara" ;
    char  target1[ 20 ] ;
```

```
    char  source2[ ] = "Folks!" ;
    char  target2[ 30 ] = "Hello" ;
    char  string1[ ] = "Jerry" ;
    char  string2[ ] = "Ferry" ;
    int  i, j, k ;

    len = strlen ( str ) ;
    printf ( "string = %s length = %d\n", str, len1 ) ;

    strcpy ( target1, source1 ) ;
    printf ( "source string = %s\n", source1 ) ;
    printf ( "target string = %s\n", target1 ) ;

    strcat ( target2, source2 ) ;
    printf ( "source string = %s\n", source2 ) ;
    printf ( "target string = %s\n", target2 ) ;

    i = strcmp ( string1, "Jerry" ) ;
    j = strcmp ( string1, string2 ) ;
    k = strcmp ( string1, "Jerry boy" ) ;
    printf ( "%d %d %d\n", i, j, k ) ;

    return 0 ;
}
```

The output of the above program on execution would be as follows:

```
string = Bamboozled length = 10
source string = Sayonara
target string = Sayonara
source string = Folks!
target string = HelloFolks!
0 4 -32
```

Note that, the function **strlen( )** returns the length of the string passed to it. While calculating the length, it does not count '\0'. The **strcpy( )** function copies the contents of source string into target string. The **strcat( )** function adds the source string at the end of the target string. For example, "Hello" and "Folks!" on concatenation would result into a string "HelloFolks!". The **strcmp( )** function compares two strings to find out whether they are same or different. The two strings are compared character by character until there is a mismatch or end of one of the strings is reached, whichever occurs first. If the two strings are identical, **strcmp( )** returns a value zero. If they are not, it returns the numeric difference between the ASCII values of the first non-matching pair of characters.

Chapter 7: Strings

While using the standard library string functions it is necessary to include the file "string.h" at the top. This file contains the prototypes of string library functions.

Two-Dimensional Array of Characters

In the last Chapter, we saw several examples of 2-dimensional integer arrays. Let's now look at a similar entity, but one dealing with characters. Our example program asks you to type your name. When you do so, it checks your name against a master list to see if you are worthy of entry to the palace. Here is the program.

```
# include <stdio.h>
# include <string.h>
# define FOUND 1
# define NOTFOUND 0
int main( )
{
    char  masterlist[ 6 ][ 10 ] = {
                            "akshay",
                            "parag",
                            "raman",
                            "srinivas",
                            "gopal",
                            "rajesh"
                        } ;
    int  i, flag, a ;
    char  yourname[ 10 ] ;

    printf ( "Enter your name " ) ;
    scanf ( "%s", yourname ) ;

    flag = NOTFOUND ;
    for ( i = 0 ; i <= 5 ; i++ )
    {
        a = strcmp ( &masterlist[ i ][ 0 ], yourname ) ;
        if ( a == 0 )
        {
            printf ( "Welcome, you can enter the palace\n" ) ;
            flag = FOUND ;
            break ;
        }
    }
    if ( flag == NOTFOUND )
        printf ( "Sorry, you are a trespasser\n" ) ;
```

```
        return 0 ;
}
```

The output of the above program for two sample runs would be as follows:

Enter your name dinesh
Sorry, you are a trespasser
Enter your name raman
Welcome, you can enter the palace

Notice how the two-dimensional character array has been initialized. The order of the subscripts in the array declaration is important. The first subscript gives the number of names in the array, while the second subscript gives the length of each item in the array.

Instead of initializing names, had these names been supplied from the keyboard, the program segment would have looked like this...

```
for ( i = 0 ; i <= 5 ; i++ )
    scanf ( "%s", &masterlist[ i ][ 0 ] ) ;
```

While comparing the strings through **strcmp( )**, note that the addresses of the strings are being passed to **strcmp( )**. As seen in the last section, if the two strings match, **strcmp( )** would return a value 0, otherwise it would return a non-zero value.

The variable **flag** is used to keep a record of whether the control did reach inside the if or not. To begin with, we set **flag** to NOTFOUND. Later through the loop, if the names match, **flag** is set to FOUND. When the control reaches beyond the **for** loop, if **flag** is still set to NOTFOUND, it means none of the names in the **masterlist[ ][ ]** matched with the one supplied from the keyboard.

Sample Programs

(a) To uniquely identify a book a 10-digit ISBN number is used. The rightmost digit is a checksum digit. This digit is determined from the other 9 digits using the condition that $d_1 + 2d_2 + 3d_3 + ... + 10d_{10}$ must be a multiple of 11 (where d_i denotes the ith digit from the right). The checksum digit d_1 can be any value from 0 to 10: the ISBN convention is to use the value X to denote 10. Write a program that receives a 10-digit integer, computes the checksum, and reports whether the ISBN number is correct or not.

Program:

Chapter 7: Strings

```c
/* Check correctness of ISBN number */
#include <stdio.h>
#include <string.h>

int main( )
{
    char str[ 11 ] ;
    int i, j, sum ;

    printf ( "Enter 10 digit ISBN number: " ) ;
    scanf ( "%s", str ) ;

    j = 2 ;
    sum = 0 ;
    for ( i = 8 ; i >= 0 ; i-- )
    {
        sum = sum + ( str [ i ] - '0' ) * j ;
        j++ ;
    }

    for ( i = 0 ; i <= 9 ; i++ )
    {
        if ( ( sum + i ) % 11 == 0 )
            break ;
    }

    if ( i == str[ 9 ] - '0' )
        printf ( "ISBN Number is verified and found to be correct\n" ) ;
    else
        printf ( "Checksum error in ISBN Number\n" ) ;

    return 0 ;
}
```

(b) Write a program that generates and prints the Fibonacci words of order 0 through 5. If f(0) = "a", f(1) = "b", f(2) = "ba", f(3) = "bab", f(4) = "babba", etc.

Program:

```c
/* Generate Fibonacci words of order 0 through 5 */
#include <stdio.h>
#include <string.h>
```

```c
int main( )
{
    char str[ 50 ] ;
    char lastbutoneterm[ 50 ] = "A" ;
    char lastterm[ 50 ] = "B" ;
    int i ;

    for ( i = 1 ; i <= 5 ; i++ )
    {
        strcpy ( str, lastterm ) ;
        strcat ( str, lastbutoneterm ) ;
        printf ( "% s\n", str ) ;
        strcpy ( lastbutoneterm, lastterm );
        strcpy ( lastterm, str ) ;
    }

    return 0 ;
}
```

(c) Write a program to sort a set of names stored in an array in alphabetical order.

Program:

```c
/* To sort strings alphabetically */
# include <stdio.h>
#include <string.h>
int main( )
{
    char str[ ][ 20 ] = {
                        "Rajesh",
                        "Ashish",
                        "Milind",
                        "Pushkar",
                        "Akash"
                       } ;

    char t ;
    int i, j, k ;

    for ( i = 0 ; i < 5 ; i++ )
    {
        for  ( j = i + 1 ; j < 5 ; j++ )
```

```
        {
            if ( ( strcmp ( str[ i ], str[ j ] ) ) > 0 )
            {
                for ( k = 0 ; k <= 19 ; k++ )
                {
                    t = str[ i ][ k ] ;
                    str[ i ][ k ] = str[ j ][ k ] ;
                    str[ j ][ k ] = t ;
                }
            }
        }
    }

    for ( i = 0 ; i < 5 ; i++ )
        printf ( "\n% s", str[ i ] ) ;

    return 0 ;
}
```

Things to Remember

(a) A string is nothing but an array of characters terminated by '\0'.

(b) Being an array, all the characters of a string are stored in contiguous memory locations.

(c) **scanf( )** and **printf( )** can be used to input/output strings.

(d) Strings can be operated upon using several standard library functions like **strlen( )**, **strcpy( )**, **strcat( )** and **strcmp( )**.

Exercise

[A] Fill in the blanks:

(a) "A" is a _____ whereas 'A' is a _____.

(b) A string is terminated by a _____ character, which is written as _____.

(c) The array **char name[10]** can consist of a maximum of _____ characters.

(d) The array elements are always stored in _____ memory locations.

(e) The file _____ should be #included while using string library functions.

[B] State whether the following statements are True or False:

(a) A string constant is a one-dimensional array of characters terminated by a null ('\0').

(b) The **strcmp( )** function is used to compare two strings.

(c) The **strlen( )** function counts the '\0' present at the end of string while reporting its length.

(d) To store 10 strings in memory 10 character arrays should be used.

[C] Attempt the following:

(a) Write a program to delete all vowels from a sentence. Assume that the sentence is not more than 80 characters long.

(b) Write a program that takes a set of names of individuals and abbreviates the first, middle and other names except the last name by their first letter.

(c) Write a program to reverse the strings stored in the following 2D array of characters:

```
char  str[ ][ 25 ] = {
            "To err is human...",
            "But to really mess things up...",
            "One needs to know C!!"
         };
```

8 Structures

- Why use Structures?
    Declaring a Structure
    Accessing Structure Elements
- Array of Structures
- Additional Features of Structures
- Uses of Structures
- Things to Remember
- Exercise

Which mechanic is good enough who knows how to repair only one type of vehicle? None. Same thing is true about C language. It would not have been so popular had it been able to handle only all **int**s, or all **float**s or all **char**s at a time. In fact, when we handle real world data, we do not usually deal with little atoms of information by themselves—things like integers, characters and such. Instead, we deal with entities that are collections of things, each thing having its own attributes, just as the entity we call a 'book' is a collection of things, such as title, author, call number, publisher, number of pages, date of publication, etc. As you can see, all this data is dissimilar, for example, author is a string, whereas number of pages is an integer. For dealing with such collections, C provides a data type called 'structure'. A structure gathers together, different atoms of information that comprise a given entity. And structure is the topic of this Chapter.

Why use Structures?

We have seen earlier how ordinary variables can hold one piece of information and how arrays can hold a number of pieces of information of the same data type. These two data types can handle a great variety of situations. But quite often we deal with entities that are collection of dissimilar data types.

For example, suppose you want to store data about a book. You might want to store its name (a string), its price (a float) and number of pages in it (an int). If data about say three such books is to be stored, then we can follow two approaches:

(a) Construct individual arrays, one for storing names, another for storing prices and still another for storing number of pages.

(b) Use a structure variable.

Let us examine these two approaches one by one. For the sake of programming convenience, assume that the names of books would be single character long. Let us begin with a program that uses arrays.

```
# include <stdio.h>
int main( )
{
    char name[ 3 ] ;
    float price[ 3 ] ;
    int pages[ 3 ], i ;

    printf ( "Enter names, prices and no. of pages of 3 books\n" ) ;
```

Chapter 8: Structures

```
    for ( i = 0 ; i <= 2 ; i++ )
        scanf ( "%c%f%d", &name[ i ], &price[ i ], &pages[ i ] ) ;

    printf ( "\nAnd this is what you entered\n" ) ;
    for ( i = 0 ; i <= 2 ; i++ )
        printf ( "%c%f%d\n", name[ i ], price[ i ], pages[ i ] ) ;
    return 0 ;
}
```

The output of the above program when executed would be as follows:

```
Enter names, prices and no. of pages of 3 books
A 100.00 354
C 256.50 682
F 233.70 512

And this is what you entered
A 100.000000 354
C 256.500000 682
F 233.700000 512
```

This approach, no doubt, allows you to store names, prices and number of pages. But as you must have realized, it is an unwieldy approach that obscures the fact that you are dealing with a group of characteristics related to a single entity—the book.

The program becomes more difficult to handle as the number of items relating to the book goes on increasing. For example, we would be required to use a number of arrays, if we also decide to store name of the publisher, date of purchase of book, etc. To solve this problem, C provides a special data type—the structure.

A structure contains a number of data types grouped together. These data types may or may not be of the same type. The following example illustrates the use of this data type.

```
# include <stdio.h>
int main( )
{
    struct book
    {
        char  name ;
        float price ;
        int   pages ;
    } ;
    struct book b1, b2, b3 ;
```

```
    printf ( "Enter names, prices & no. of pages of 3 books\n" ) ;
    scanf ( "%c%f%d", &b1.name, &b1.price, &b1.pages ) ;
    scanf ( "%c%f%d", &b2.name, &b2.price, &b2.pages ) ;
    scanf ( "%c%f%d", &b3.name, &b3.price, &b3.pages ) ;
    printf ( "And this is what you entered\n" ) ;
    printf ( "%c%f%d\n", b1.name, b1.price, b1.pages ) ;
    printf ( "%c%f%d\n", b2.name, b2.price, b2.pages ) ;
    printf ( "%c%f%d\n", b3.name, b3.price, b3.pages ) ;
    return 0 ;
}
```

The output of the above program when executed would be as follows:

```
Enter names, prices and no. of pages of 3 books
A  100.00  354
C  256.50  682
F  233.70  512
And this is what you entered
A  100.000000  354
C  256.500000  682
F  233.700000  512
```

This program demonstrates two fundamental aspects of structures:

(a) Declaration of a structure
(b) Accessing of structure elements

Let us now look at these concepts one by one.

Declaring a Structure

In our example program, the following statement declares the structure type:

```
struct book
{
    char  name ;
    float price ;
    int  pages ;
} ;
```

Chapter 8: Structures

This statement defines a new data type called **struct book**. Each variable of this data type will consist of a character variable called **name**, a float variable called **price** and an integer variable called **pages**. The general form of a structure declaration statement is given below.

```
struct <structure name>
{
    structure element 1 ;
    structure element 2 ;
    structure element 3 ;
    ......
    ......
};
```

Once the new structure data type has been defined, one or more variables can be declared to be of that type. For example, the variables **b1, b2, b3** can be declared to be of the type **struct book**, as,

struct book b1, b2, b3 ;

This statement sets aside space in memory. It makes available space to hold all the elements in the structure—in this case, 7 bytes—one for **name**, four for **price** and two for **pages**. These bytes are always in adjacent memory locations.

If we so desire, we can combine the declaration of the structure type and the structure variables in one statement.

For example,

```
struct book
{
    char  name ;
    float price ;
    int   pages ;
};
struct book  b1, b2, b3 ;
```

is same as...

```
struct book
{
    char  name ;
    float price ;
```

```
        int pages ;
} b1, b2, b3 ;
```

or even...

```
struct
{
    char name ;
    float price ;
    int pages ;
} b1, b2, b3 ;
```

Like primary variables and arrays, structure variables can also be initialized where they are declared. The format used is quite similar to that used to initialize arrays.

```
struct book
{
    char name[ 10 ] ;
    float price ;
    int pages ;
} ;
struct book  b1 = { "Basic", 130.00, 550 } ;
struct book  b2 = { "Physics", 150.80, 800 } ;
struct book  b3 = { 0 } ;
```

Note the following points while declaring a structure type:

(a) The closing brace in the structure type declaration must be followed by a semicolon.

(b) It is important to understand that a structure type declaration does not tell the compiler to reserve any space in memory. All a structure declaration does is, it defines the 'form' of the structure.

(c) Usually structure type declaration appears at the top of the source code file, before any variables or functions are defined. In very large programs they are usually put in a separate header file, and the file is included (using the preprocessor directive #include) in whichever program we want to use this structure type.

(d) If a structure variable is initiated to a value { 0 }, then all its elements are set to value 0, as in **b3** above. This is a handy way of initializing structure variables. In absence of this, we would have been required to initialize each individual element to a value 0.

Chapter 8: Structures

Accessing Structure Elements

Having declared the structure type and the structure variables, let us see how the elements of the structure can be accessed.

In arrays, we can access individual elements of an array using a subscript. Structures use a different scheme. They use a dot (.) operator. So to refer to **pages** of the structure defined in our sample program, we have to use,

b1.pages

Similarly, to refer to **price**, we would use,

b1.price

Note that before the dot, there must always be a structure variable and after the dot, there must always be a structure element.

Array of Structures

Our sample program showing usage of structure is rather simple minded. All it does is, it receives values into various structure elements and output these values. But that's all we intended to do—show how structure types are created, how structure variables are declared and how individual elements of a structure variable are referenced.

In our sample program, to store data of 100 books, we would be required to use 100 different structure variables from **b1** to **b100**, which is definitely not very convenient. A better approach would be to use an array of structures. Following program shows how to use an array of structures:

```
/* Usage of an array of structures */
# include <stdio.h>
void linkfloat( ) ;
int main( )
{
    struct book
    {
        char name ;
        float price ;
        int pages ;
    } ;
```

```c
    struct book  b[ 100 ] ;
    int  i ;

    for ( i = 0 ; i <= 99 ; i++ )
    {
        printf ( "Enter name, price and pages " ) ;
        fflush ( stdin ) ;
        scanf ( "%c%f%d", &b[ i ].name, &b[ i ].price, &b[ i ].pages ) ;
    }

    for ( i = 0 ; i <= 99 ; i++ )
        printf ( "%c%f%d\n", b[ i ].name, b[ i ].price, b[ i ].pages ) ;

    return 0 ;
}

void linkfloat( )
{
    float a = 0, *b ;
    b = &a ;  /* cause emulator to be linked */
    a = *b ;  /* suppress the warning - variable not used */
}
```

Now a few comments about the program:

(a) Notice how the array of structures is declared,

   struct book b[100] ;

   This provides space in memory for 100 structures of the type **struct book**.

(b) The syntax we use to reference each element of the array **b** is similar to the syntax used for arrays of **int**s and **char**s. For example, we refer to zeroth book's price as **b[0].price**. Similarly, we refer first book's pages as **b[1].pages**.

(c) It should be appreciated what careful thought Dennis Ritchie has put into C language. He first defined array as a collection of similar elements; then realized that dissimilar data types that are often found in real life cannot be handled using arrays, therefore created a new data type called structure. But even using structures, programming convenience could not be achieved, because a lot of variables (**b1** to **b100** for storing data about hundred books) needed to be handled. Therefore, he allowed us to create an array of structures; an array of similar data types which themselves are a collection of dissimilar data types. Hats off to the genius!

(d) In an array of structures, all elements of the array are stored in adjacent memory locations. Since each element of this array is a structure, and since all structure elements are always stored in adjacent locations, you can very well visualize the arrangement of array of structures in memory. In our example, **b[0]**'s **name**, **price** and **pages** in memory would be immediately followed by **b[1]**'s **name**, **price** and **pages**, and so on.

(e) What is the function **linkfloat( )** doing here? If you do not define it, you are likely to get an error "Floating Point Formats Not Linked" with many C Compilers. What causes this error to occur? When parsing our source file, if the compiler encounters a reference to the address of a float, it sets a flag to have the linker link in the floating-point emulator. A floating-point emulator is used to manipulate floating-point numbers in functions like **scanf( )** and **atof( )**. There are some cases in which the reference to the **float** is a bit obscure and the compiler does not detect the need for the emulator. The most common is using **scanf( )** to read a **float** in an array of structures as shown in our program.

How can we force the formats to be linked? That's where the **linkfloat( )** function comes in. It forces linking of the floating-point emulator into an application. There is no need to call this function, just define it anywhere in your program.

Additional Features of Structures

Let us now explore the intricacies of structures with a view of programming convenience. We would highlight these intricacies with suitable examples:

(a) The values of a structure variable can be assigned to another structure variable of the same type using the assignment operator. It is not necessary to copy the structure elements piece-meal. Obviously, programmers prefer assignment to piece-meal copying. This is shown in the following example:

```
# include <stdio.h>
# include <string.h>
int main( )
{
    struct employee
    {
        char  name[ 10 ] ;
        int  age ;
```

```
        float salary ;
    } ;
    struct employee e1 = { "Sanjay", 30, 5500.50 } ;
    struct employee e2, e3 ;

    /* piece-meal copying */
    strcpy ( e2.name, e1.name ) ;  /* e2.name = e1. name is wrong */
    e2.age = e1.age ;
    e2.salary = e1.salary ;

    /* copying all elements at one go */
    e3 = e2 ;

    printf ( "%s %d %f\n", e1.name, e1.age, e1.salary ) ;
    printf ( "%s %d %f\n", e2.name, e2.age, e2.salary ) ;
    printf ( "%s %d %f\n", e3.name, e3.age, e3.salary ) ;
    return 0 ;
}
```

The output of the above program when executed would be as follows:

Sanjay 30 5500.500000
Sanjay 30 5500.500000
Sanjay 30 5500.500000

Ability to copy the contents of all structure elements of one variable into the corresponding elements of another structure variable is rather surprising, since C does not allow assigning the contents of one array to another just by equating the two. As we saw earlier, for copying arrays, we have to copy the contents of the array element by element.

This copying of all structure elements at one go has been possible only because the structure elements are stored in contiguous memory locations. Had this not been so, we would have been required to copy structure variables element by element. And who knows, had this been so, structures would not have become popular at all.

(b) One structure can be nested within another structure. Using this facility, complex data types can be created. The following program shows nested structures at work:

```
# include <stdio.h>
int main( )
{
    struct address
```

Chapter 8: Structures **117**

```
    {
        char  phone[ 15 ] ;
        char  city[ 25 ] ;
        int  pin ;
    } ;

    struct emp
    {
        char  name[ 25 ] ;
        struct address  a ;
    } ;
    struct emp  e = { "jeru", "531046", "nagpur", 10 };

    printf ( "name = %s phone = %s\n", e.name, e.a.phone ) ;
    printf ( "city = %s pin = %d\n", e.a.city, e.a.pin ) ;
    return 0 ;
}
```

The output of the above program when executed would be as follows:

name = jeru phone = 531046
city = nagpur pin = 10

Notice the method used to access the element of a structure that is part of another structure. For this, the dot operator is used twice, as in the expression,

e.a.pin or e.a.city

Of course, the nesting process need not stop at this level. We can nest a structure within a structure, within another structure, which is in still another structure and so on... till the time we can comprehend the structure ourselves. Such construction, however, gives rise to variable names that can be surprisingly self-descriptive, for example:

maruti.engine.bolt.large.qty

This clearly signifies that we are referring to the quantity of large sized bolts that fit on an engine of a maruti car.

(c) Like an ordinary variable, a structure variable can also be passed to a function. This is shown in the following program:

```
# include <stdio.h>
```

```c
struct book
{
    char  name[ 25 ] ;
    char  author[ 25 ] ;
    int  callno ;
} ;
void display ( struct book ) ;

int main( )
{
    struct book  b1 = { "Let us C", "YPK", 101 } ;
    display ( b1 ) ;
    return 0 ;
}

void display ( struct book  b )
{
    printf ( "%s %s %d\n", b.name, b.author, b.callno ) ;
}
```

And here is the output...

Let us C YPK 101

Note that here the calling of function **display( )** becomes quite compact,

display (b1) ;

Having collected what is being passed to the **display( )** function, the question comes, how do we define the formal arguments in the function. We cannot say,

struct book b1 ;

because the data type **struct book** is not known to the function **display( )**. Therefore, it becomes necessary to declare the structure type **struct book** outside **main( )**, so that it becomes known to all functions in the program.

Uses of Structures

Where are structures useful? The immediate application that comes to the mind is Database Management. That is, to maintain data about employees in an organization, books in a library, items in a store, financial accounting transactions in a company etc.

Chapter 8: Structures

But mind you, use of structures stretches much beyond database management. They can be used for a variety of purposes like:

(a) Changing the size of the cursor
(b) Clearing the contents of the screen
(c) Placing the cursor at an appropriate position on screen
(d) Drawing any graphics shape on the screen
(e) Receiving a key from the keyboard
(f) Checking the memory size of the computer
(g) Finding out the list of equipment attached to the computer
(h) Formatting a floppy
(i) Hiding a file from the directory
(j) Displaying the directory of a disk
(k) Sending the output to printer
(l) Interacting with the mouse

And that is certainly a very impressive list! At least impressive enough to make you realize how important a data type a structure is and to be thorough with it if you intend to program any of the above applications.

Things to Remember

(a) A structure is usually used when we wish to store dissimilar data together.

(b) Structure elements can be accessed through a structure variable using a dot (.) operator.

(c) All elements of one structure variable can be assigned to another structure variable using the assignment (=) operator.

(d) It is possible to pass a structure variable to a function.

(e) It is possible to create an array of structures.

Exercise

[A] Answer the following:

(a) Ten float values are to be stored in memory. What would you prefer, an array or a structure?

(b) Given the statement,

maruti.engine.bolts = 25 ;

which of the following is True?

1. Structure bolts is nested within structure engine.
2. Structure engine is nested within structure maruti.
3. Structure maruti is nested within structure engine.
4. Structure maruti is nested within structure bolts.

[B] State whether the following statements are True or False:

(a) All structure elements are stored in contiguous memory locations.

(b) An array should be used to store dissimilar elements, and a structure to store similar elements.

(c) In an array of structures, not only are all structures stored in contiguous memory locations, but the elements of individual structures are also stored in contiguous locations.

[C] Attempt the following:

(a) Create a structure to specify data on students given below:

Roll number, Name, Department, Course, Year of joining

Assume that there are not more than 450 students in the college.
1. Write a function to print names of all students who joined in a particular year.
2. Write a function to print the data of a student whose roll number is received by the function.

(b) Create a structure to specify data of customers in a bank. The data to be stored is: Account number, Name, Balance in account. Assume maximum of 200 customers in the bank.

1. Write a function to print the Account number and Name of each customer with balance below ₹ 100.

2. If a customer requests for withdrawal or deposit, it is given in the form:

 Acct. no, amount, code (1 for deposit, 0 for withdrawal)

 Write a program to give a message, "The balance is insufficient for the specified withdrawal", if on withdrawal the balance falls below ₹ 100.

(c) There is a structure called **employee** that holds information like employee code, name and date of joining. Write a program to create an array of structures and enter some data into it. Then ask the user to enter current date. Display the names of those employees whose tenure is greater than equal to 3 years.

9 Graphics Programming

- The First Graphics Program
- All Lines are Not Same
- Drawing and Filling Shapes
- Filling Regular and Non-Regular Shapes
- Outputting Text
- A Bit of Animation
- Things to Remember
- Exercise

Computer graphics is one of the most powerful and interesting facet of computers. There is a lot that you can do in graphics apart from drawing figures of various shapes. All video games, animation, multimedia predominantly works using computer graphics. The intention of this Chapter is to give you a feel of how some of these things are achieved in C.

The First Graphics Program

Let me first show you our first graphics program to draw different shapes on the screen. Once you take a look at the program go through the explanation that follows it very thoroughly. Here is the program.

```c
# include <graphics.h>
int main( )
{
    int gd = DETECT, gm, x, y ;
    int array[ ] = { 540, 220, 590, 270, 570, 320, 510, 320, 490, 270, 540, 220 } ;

    initgraph ( &gd, &gm, "c:\\tc\\bgi" ) ;

    x = getmaxx( ) ;
    y = getmaxy( ) ;

    setcolor ( WHITE ) ;
    rectangle ( x / 30, y / 20, x / 5, y / 4 ) ;
    outtextxy ( x / 30 + 15, y / 8 + 5, "Rectangle" ) ;

    circle ( x / 2, y / 6, 75 ) ;
    putpixel ( x / 2, y / 6, WHITE ) ;
    outtextxy ( x / 2 - textwidth ( "Circle" ) / 2, y / 6 + 10, "Circle" ) ;

    arc ( x / 1.2, y / 6, 300, 90, 80 ) ;
    outtextxy ( x / 1.2, y / 6, "Arc" ) ;

    line ( x / 30, 10 * y / 15, x / 6, 10 * y / 15 ) ;
    outtextxy ( x / 30 + 10, 10 * y / 15 + 10, "Line" ) ;

    ellipse ( x / 2, 10 * y / 17, 0, 360, 100, 50 ) ;
    putpixel ( x / 2, 10 * y / 17, WHITE ) ;
    outtextxy ( x / 2 - textwidth ( "Ellipse" ) / 2, 10 * y / 17 + 10, "Ellipse" ) ;

    drawpoly ( 6, array ) ;
    outtextxy ( 515, 270, "Polygon" ) ;
```

```
        getch( ) ;
        closegraph( ) ;
        restorecrtmode( ) ;
}
```

When we start drawing any graphics on the screen we need a header file called graphics.h and a library file called graphics.lib. The header file contains definitions and explanations of all the functions and constants we will need, whereas the graphics functions are kept in the graphics library file. Both these files are provided as part of Turbo C.

First thing that we need to do before we can carry out any drawing activity is, switch over to the graphics mode. This is not simple, since depending on the adapter and monitor that is installed on your computer, only some of the several graphics modes may be available to you. These modes have been given numbers. Out of all the modes available, we would like to switch over to the one which offers the best possible resolution.

Did we say resolution? Well, the number of dots or picture elements (pixels) available to us on the screen in the graphics mode, is known as the resolution. The greater the number of dots, the higher the resolution. Simply put, this means that more the dots available, clearer would be our picture.

To switch over to the graphics mode that offers the best resolution, we need to call the function **initgraph( )**. It figures out the best resolution and puts the number corresponding to that mode in the variable **gm**. The **gm** number tells us which monitor we are using, and its resolution and the colors that are available.

Note that I have written the programs in this Chapter on a color monitor driven by a Video Graphics Array (VGA), the maximum resolution of which is 640 x 480 (i.e., 640 pixels from left to right and 480 pixels from top to bottom). For other adapters, I expect you to make the necessary changes in the programs.

In **gd**, we should set up a value **DETECT**. As a result, **initgraph( )** would find out which driver file is needed for our monitor and load that file in memory. The third parameter "C:\\tc\\bgi" indicates where the driver file should be searched.

So much about the graphics modes and changing over to the appropriate graphics mode. Two things happen the moment we change over to the graphics mode. Firstly, the cursor disappears since the graphics modes do not support the conventional cursor. Secondly, a coordinate system is established whereby the top left corner of the screen is treated as origin **(0, 0)**. As usual, the X-axis goes horizontally across, and the Y-axis goes vertically downward.

Once into the graphics mode we can set the color in which drawing can be done. This is achieved using the **setcolor()** function, for example **setcolor (RED)**. In place of RED we can use any other color like BLACK, BLUE, GREEN, CYAN, MAGENTA, BROWN, ELLOW, WHITE, etc.

Before drawing the rectangle we have used two functions **getmaxx( )** and **getmaxy( )**. These fetch the maximum x and y coordinates for the chosen graphics mode. The basic tools that we will need for drawing shapes are functions like **putpixel( ), line( ), circle( ), ellipse( ), arc( )** and **drawpoly( )**. All these functions have been used in our program. Their general form is shown in Table 9.1.

Function	Meaning
putpixel (x1, y1) ;	Lits the pixel at *(x1, y1)*.
line (x1, y1, x2,. y2) ;	Draws a line from *(x1, y1)* to *(x2, y2)*.
circle (xc, yc, rad) ;	Draws a circle with center *(xc, yc)* and radius *rad*.
rectangle (x1, y1, x2, y2) ;	Draws a rectangle with *(x1, y1)* and *(x2, y2)* as corners.
ellipse (xc, yc, start, end, xrad, yrad) ;	Draws an ellipse with *(xc, yc)* as center with *xrad* and *rad* as x and y radius. If *start* is 0 and *end* is 180 only the upper half of the ellipse is drawn.
arc (xc, yc, start, end, rad);	Draws an arc with *(xc,yc)* as center, *rad* as radius and *start* and *end* as the starting and ending angles.

Table 9.1 Various drawing functions

All Lines are not Same

In the previous program, we drew a line using the **line( )** function. The coordinates passed to this functions were with respect to the origin **(0, 0)**, represented by the pixel at the top-left corner of the screen. Another way to draw a line is to use a combination of two functions **moveto( )** and **lineto( )**. The **moveto( )** function moves the CP to the specified coordinates. What is this CP? It stands for Current Position. When we initialise the graphics system CP is at the origin. On executing some drawing functions CP changes, whereas in others it doesn't. For example, after drawing a line using the **line( )** function CP doesn't change, whereas, on drawing a line using the function **lineto( )** the CP changes to the end point of the line drawn.

It is also possible to draw a line relative to a particular point on the screen using the **linerel( )** function. The coordinates passed to **linerel( )** specify where we want the line to

Chapter 9: Graphics Programming

end using the said point as our origin. To reach the starting point we can use either the function **moveto( )** or **moverel( )**. The first function moves the CP to the given coordinates with **(0, 0)** as the origin, whereas, the second moves the CP by a relative distance from its current position. The following program uses the three methods mentioned above to draw lines on the screen:

```
#include <graphics.h>
#include <stdlib.h>
#include <stdio.h>
#include <conio.h>
int main( )
{
    int gd = DETECT, gm ;
    char msg[ 80 ] ;

    initgraph ( &gd, &gm, "c:\\tc\\bgi" ) ;

    outtextxy ( 100, 0, "Demonstration of Moveto, Lineto, Moverel, Linerel" ) ;
    rectangle ( 0, 10, 639, 479 ) ;

    line ( 100, 50, 100, 350 ) ;  /* draws a line */

    moveto ( 300, 50 ) ;  /* moves the CP */
    lineto ( 300, 350 ) ;  /* draws a line up to the point */

    moverel ( 200, -300 ) ;  /* moves the CP by relative distance from its current position */
    linerel ( 0, 300 ) ;  /* draws a line from the CP to a point a relative
                            distance away from the current value of CP */

    outtextxy ( 104, 50, "( 100, 50 )" ) ;
    outtextxy ( 104, 350, "( 100, 350 )" ) ;
    outtextxy ( 90, 375, "Line" ) ;

    outtextxy ( 304, 50, "( 300, 50 )" ) ;
    outtextxy ( 304, 350, "( 300, 350 )" ) ;
    outtextxy ( 280, 375, "Moveto, Lineto" ) ;

    outtextxy ( 504, 50, "( 500, 50 )" ) ;
    outtextxy ( 504, 350, "(-500, 350 )" ) ;
    outtextxy ( 480, 375, "Moverel, Linerel" ) ;

    getch( ) ;
    closegraph( ) ;
```

```
        restorecrtmode( ) ;
}
```

This program draws three lines. The first line has been drawn using the usual **line( )** function. The second one has been drawn using the **moveto( )**, **lineto( )** functions. Note that for drawing this line we have reached our starting point **(300, 50)** by calling the **moveto( )** function and then drawn a line up to **(300, 350)** using the **lineto( )** function. This shifts the C.P. to **(300, 350)**. The third line is drawn by first shifting the CP from its current position by a relative distance of 200 pixels to the right and 300 pixels up using the **moverel( )** function. Next the line is drawn using the function **linerel( )**, once again using the relative distances.

Drawing and Filling Shapes

With the basics over, let us now get into more complicated stuff. Stuff which would permit us to draw bars and then fill them up with different patterns. Here is a program which shows how this can be achieved.

```
# include "graphics.h"
int main( )
{
    int gd = DETECT, gm, maxx, maxy, x = 40, y = 40, fst ;
    char str[ 40 ] ;

    char *pattern[ ] = {
                    "EMPTY_FILL", "SOLID_FILL", "LINE_FILL", "LTSLASH_FILL",
                    "SLASH_FILL", "BKSLASH_FILL", "LTBKSLASH_FILL", "HATCH_FILL",
                    "XHATCH_FILL", "INTERLEAVE_FILL", "WIDE_DOT_FILL",
                    "CLOSE_DOT_FILL", "USER_FILL"
                } ;

    initgraph ( &gd, &gm, "c:\\tc\\bgi" ) ;

    maxx = getmaxx( ) ;
    maxy = getmaxy( ) ;
    rectangle ( 0, 10, maxx, maxy ) ;

    setcolor ( WHITE ) ;
    outtextxy ( 175, 0, "Pre-defined Fill styles" ) ;

    /* display different predefined fill styles */
    for ( fst = 0 ; fst < 12 ; fst++ )
```

Chapter 9: Graphics Programming

```
        {
                setfillstyle ( fst, MAGENTA ) ;
                bar ( x, y, x + 80, y + 80 ) ;
                rectangle ( x, y, x + 80, y + 80 ) ;

                itoa ( fst, str, 10 ) ;
                outtextxy ( x, y + 100, str ) ;
                outtextxy ( x, y + 110, pattern[ fst ] ) ;

                x = x + 150 ;
                if ( x > 490 )
                {
                    y = y + 150 ;
                    x = 40 ;
                }
        }

        getch( ) ;
        closegraph( ) ;
        restorecrtmode( ) ;
}
```

In this program, we have drawn 12 rectangles and filled them with the available fill patterns. To achieve this we have first used the **bar( )** function to fill a rectangular area with a pattern and then enclosed it by calling the **rectangle( )** function. Note that the **bar( )** function does not draw the boundary but fills the interior with the current fill pattern and current fill color, whereas the **rectangle( )** function draws the rectangle in current color but does not fill the insides of it.

Figure 9.2 shows the fill patterns defined in 'graphics.h' along with their enumerated integer values. If we want we can save the current fill pattern and current fill color through statements given below.

```
struct fillsettingstype old ;
getfillsettings ( &old ) ;
```

The **fillsettingstype** structure has been defined in 'graphics.h' as follows:

```
struct fillsettingstype
{
    int pattern ;
    int color ;
} ;
```

If saved earlier, the fill pattern and the fill color can be restored through a call to **setfillstyle()**:

setfillstyle (old.pattern, old.color) ;

Name	Value	Description
EMPTY_FILL	0	Fill with background color
SOLID_FILL	1	Solid fill
LINE_FILL	2	Fill with -------
LTSLASH_FILL	3	Fill with /////
SLASH_FILL	4	Fill with /////, thick lines
BKSLASH_FILL	5	Fill with \\\\\\, thick lines
LTBKSLASH_FILL	6	Fill with \\\\\\
HATCH_FILL	7	Light hatch fill
XHATCH_FILL	8	Heavy cross-hatch fill
INTERLEAVE_FILL	9	Interleaving line fill
WIDE_DOT_FILL	10	Widely spaced dot fill
CLOSE_DOT_FILL	11	Closely spaced dot fill
USER_FILL	12	User-defined fill pattern

Table 9.2 Fill Patterns defined in 'graphics.h'

Filling Regular and Non-Regular Shapes

To fill regular shapes like polygons and ellipses there exist standard library functions like **fillpoly( )** and **fillellipse( )**. These functions fill the polygon (or ellipse) with the current fill style and current fill color that may have been set up by calling **setfillstyle( )** or **setfillpattern( )**. However, if we are to fill non-regular shapes like the intersecting area between an overlapping triangle and circle, we have to once again take recourse to the **floodfill( )** function.

The following program draws an ellipse and a triangle, and fills them by calling the **fillellipse( )** and **fillpoly( )** functions. Next it draws an overlapping triangle and circle and fills the intersecting and non-intersecting areas by repeatedly calling the **floodfill( )** function. The parameters passed to **fillellipse( )** include coordinates of the center, X-

Chapter 9: Graphics Programming **129**

radius and Y-radius. The parameters passed to **drawpoly( )** and **fillpoly( )** are same: the number of points used to build the polygon and the base address of the array containing the coordinates of these points.

```
# include <graphics.h>
int main( )
{
    int gd = DETECT, gm, maxx, maxy, x = 600, y = 450 ;
    int array[ ] = { 350, 180, 400, 80, 450, 180, 350, 180 } ;

    initgraph ( &gd, &gm, "c:\\tc\\bgi" ) ;

    maxx = getmaxx( ) ;
    maxy = getmaxy( ) ;
    rectangle ( 0, 20, maxx, maxy ) ;
    setcolor ( WHITE ) ;
    outtextxy ( 150, 10, "Fill Figures using different functions" ) ;
    ellipse ( x / 4, 10 * y / 35, 0, 360, 100, 50 ) ;

    outtextxy ( x / 4 - textwidth ( "Ellipse" ) / 2, 10 * y / 24 + 10, "Ellipse" ) ;
    setfillstyle ( SOLID_FILL, RED ) ;
    fillellipse ( x / 4, 10 * y / 35, 100, 50 ) ;

    drawpoly ( 4, array ) ;
    fillpoly ( 4, array ) ;
    outtextxy ( 370, 200, "Polygon" ) ;

    circle ( 280, 320, 70 ) ;
    line ( 190, 350, 370, 350 ) ;
    moveto ( 190, 350 ) ;
    linerel ( 100, -120 ) ;
    linerel ( 80, 120 ) ;
    outtextxy ( 210, 410, "User-defined figure" ) ;

    floodfill ( 280, 320, WHITE ) ;

    setfillstyle ( SOLID_FILL, BLUE ) ;
    floodfill ( 192, 349, WHITE ) ;
    floodfill ( 368, 349, WHITE ) ;
    floodfill ( 290, 231, WHITE ) ;

    setfillstyle ( SOLID_FILL, DARKGRAY ) ;
    floodfill ( 240, 289, WHITE ) ;
```

```
        floodfill ( 330, 289, WHITE ) ;
        floodfill ( 280, 351, WHITE ) ;

        getch( ) ;
        closegraph( ) ;
        restorecrtmode( ) ;
}
```

Outputting Text

So far we have outputted text using the function **outtextxy( )**. However, there is more to outputting text than what we have covered. The following program would put the whole issue in the right perspective:

```
# include "graphics.h"
int main( )
{
    int gd = DETECT, gm, x = 10, y, i, j ;
    char str[ ] = "Fonts" ;
    char *demo[ ] = {
                    "Default Font Demonstration",
                    "Triplex Font Demonstration",
                    "Small Font Demonstration",
                    "Sansserif Font Demonstration",
                    "Gothic Font Demonstration",
                    "Script Font Demonstration",
                    "Simplex Font Demonstration",
                    "Triplex Script Font Demonstration",
                    "Complex Font Demonstration",
                    "European Font Demonstration",
                    "Bold Font Demonstration"
                    } ;

    initgraph ( &gd, &gm, "c:\\tc\\bgi" ) ;

    setcolor ( WHITE ) ;

    for ( i = 0 ; i <= 10 ; i++ )
    {
        rectangle ( 0, 20, 639, 479 ) ;
        settextstyle ( 0, 0, 1 ) ;
        outtextxy ( 150, 10, demo[ i ] ) ;
```

Chapter 9: Graphics Programming **131**

```
        y = 30 ;
        for ( j = 1 ; j <= 4 ; j++ )
        {
            settextstyle ( i, HORIZ_DIR, j ) ;
            outtextxy ( 10, y, str ) ;
            y += ( textheight ( str ) + 10 ) ;
        }

        settextstyle ( i, VERT_DIR, 0 ) ;
        setusercharsize ( 2, 1, 3, 2 ) ;
        outtextxy ( 10, y, str ) ;

        getch( ) ;
        clearviewport( ) ;
    }

    closegraph( ) ;
    restorecrtmode( ) ;
}
```

In the earlier programs, when we used the **outtextxy( )** function the text got printed using a default font, direction and point size. The function **settextstyle( )** enables us to change the font, direction and character size. Turbo C provides us with ten fonts in addition to the default font. These are Triplex, Small, Sans Serif, Gothic, Script, Simplex, Triplex Script, Complex, European and Bold. We can output the text either horizontally (default) or vertically. And we can choose any one of the 10 point sizes of characters. For point size 1, each character is displayed in a 8 x 8 pixel rectangle. If the point size is 2 then the character is displayed using 16 x 16 pixel rectangle and so on.

The general form of **settextstyle( )** function is given below,

settextstyle (font, direction, point size) ;

In our program we have kept the direction of output horizontal and changed the font and the point size through a pair of loops. To determine the position at which the text is to be outputted each time through the loop, we have used the function **textheight( )** which determines the height of a string as per the current font. Instead of using all the 10 point sizes we have run the inner loop only four times do demonstrate four point sizes.

Once outside the inner *for* loop we have used the **setusercharsize( )** function to use a user-defined point size. This function gives you finer control over the size of the text. Its prototype looks like this.

setusercharsize (int multx, int divx, int multy, int divy) ;

The parameters passed to this function help us to specify factors by which the width and height are scaled. The default width is scaled by **multx : divx,** and the default height is scaled by **multy : divvy.** For example, to make the text twice as wide and 50% taller than the default, we have set,

multx = 2 ; divx = 1 ;
multy = 3 ; divy = 2 ;

A Bit of Animation

Drawing images is all right, what if we want to move them on the screen? This can be achieved through two functions **getimage( )** and **putimage( )**. The former reads any specified image from the screen, and the latter places it at a predetermined subsequent location, giving the illusion of movement. The following program shows how these functions can be used in tandem to move a ball on the screen:

```
# include <graphics.h>
# include <alloc.h>
main( )
{
    int gd = DETECT, gm, area, x = 25, y = 25, ch, xdirn = 1, ydirn = 1 ;
    int maxx, maxy ;
    char *buff ;

    initgraph ( &gd, &gm, "c:\\tc\\bgi" ) ;

    setcolor ( WHITE ) ;
    setfillstyle ( SOLID_FILL, RED ) ;
    circle ( 50, 50, 25 ) ;
    floodfill ( 50, 50, WHITE ) ;

    area = imagesize ( 25, 25, 75, 75 ) ;
    buff = malloc ( area ) ;
    getimage ( 25, 25, 75, 75, buff ) ;

    maxx = getmaxx( ) ;
    maxy = getmaxy( ) ;
    rectangle ( 0, 20, maxx, maxy ) ;
    outtextxy ( 250, 10, "Animation" ) ;
```

```c
while ( 1 )
{
    if ( kbhit( ) )
    {
        ch = getch( ) ;

        /* if ENTER is hit reverse the direction of movement */
        if ( ch =='\r' )
        {
            xdirn *= -1 ;
            ydirn *= -1 ;
        }
        else
        {
            if ( ch == 27 )
                break ;
        }
    }

    putimage ( x, y, buff, XOR_PUT ) ;
    delay ( 0 ) ;
    x = x + ( xdirn * 5 ) ;
    y = y + ( ydirn * 2 ) ;
    putimage ( x, y, buff, XOR_PUT ) ;

    /* check if ball touches horizontal boundaries */
    if ( x > maxx - 50 || x < 0 )
    {
        sound ( 50 ) ;
        delay ( 10 ) ;
        nosound( ) ;
        xdirn *= -1 ;
    }

    /* check if ball touches vertical boundaries */
    if ( y > maxy - 50 || y < 20 )
        {
         sound ( 50 ) ;
        delay ( 10 ) ;
        nosound( ) ;
        ydirn *= -1 ;
    }
}
```

```
getch( ) ;
closegraph( ) ;
restorecrtmode( ) ;
}
```

To begin with, we have drawn a circle and filled it with a SOLID_FILL pattern in RED color. After this, we wish to capture the image of this filled circle in memory. For this, we need to know how many bytes would be required to store the image in memory. We get this by calling **imagesize( )**, which returns the bytes required to store an image in memory. The parameters passed to **imagesize( )** are the top and bottom corners of the rectangle enclosing the circle (or the image to be stored).

The next step is to allocate memory, which is done by calling the function **malloc( )**. The address of allocated memory returned by **malloc( )** is stored in the variable **buff**. Since **buff** contains address of a **char** it is defined as **char *buff**. Such variables which contains addresses are known as pointers.

Then the function **getimage( )** is called which requires five parameters, the first four being the coordinates of the top left and bottom right of the block, and the last being the address of the memory location from where **getimage( )** will start storing the image.

The function **putimage( )** is the other side of the coin. It requires four parameters: the first two are the coordinates of the top left corner of the block, the third is the address in memory from where the image is to be retrieved, and the fourth specifies how the image should be displayed.

Having picked up the image in memory we should now erase the image from its original place and place it at a new location. This cycle should be repeated several times so that we get the impression of a ball moving on the screen. To implement this cycle of erasing-drawing-erasing, we have employed a **while** loop. Every time through the loop, the first call to **putimage( )** erases the ball and the second call draws it at a new position.

How come the same **putimage( )** can sometimes draw the image and at other times erase it? The value of the fourth argument supplied to **putimage( )** decides whether it would draw or erase. Table 9.4 summarizes the value of this argument and its significance.

Chapter 9: Graphics Programming

Argument passed	Status of image		Resultant image on screen
	Memory	Screen	
XOR_PUT	Present	Present	Erased
XOR_PUT	Present	Absent	Drawn
OR_PUT	Present	Present	Superimposed
OR_PUT	Present	Absent	Superimposed
COPY_PUT	Present	Present	Replaced
COPY_PUT	Present	Absent	Replaced

Table 9.3 Parameters used in putimage( ) function

The variables **xdirn** and **ydirn** are used to change the trajectory of movement of ball. Anytime Enter key is hit the direction in which the ball is traversing is reversed. Anytime the ball hits the boundary, the **sound( )** function is used to activate the speaker followed by **nosound( )** to stop the sound. **delay( )** serves the purpose of letting the speaker beep for sometime before it is shut out by **nosound( )**.

Things to Remember

(a) Before drawing any graphics on the screen, we need to call **initgraph( )** to initialize the graphics system.

(b) There are many library functions available in Turbo C to draw graphics on the screen.

(c) Lines can be drawn either using absolute coordinates or using relative coordinates.

(d) Regular shapes can be filled using different fill patterns and colors.

(e) Non-regular shapes can be filled using the **floodfill( )** function.

(f) In graphics mode, text can be displayed in different fonts.

(g) It is possible to animate any drawing using the **getimage( )** and **putimage( )** functions.

Exercise

[A] State whether the following statements are True or False:

(a) The **initgraph( )** function is available in graphics.h library.

(b) The **lineto( )** function moves the current position to the specified coordinates.

(c) The general form of **settextstyle( )** function is **settextstyle (font, direction, point size) ;** .

[B] Fill in the blanks:

(a) Prototype declarations of all graphics related functions are present in the file _____ .

(b) The _____ function enables us to change the font, direction and point size.

(c) The _____ function is used to fill a non-regular shape.

[C] Answer the following:

(a) Write a program to draw 10 concentric circles on the screen of suitable diameters. Fill each circle with a different color.

(b) Write a program to display on the screen your name in different fonts.

(c) Write a program do draw image of a human face and to animate it to move in any direction on the screen.

(d) Write a program to draw a 4-petalled lotus on the screen. Fill it with suitable colors.